Betrayed

Lyndsey Harris was the winner of the Richard & Judy competition TRUE. The series was executive produced by Simon and Amanda Ross, and produced by Gareth Jones and Zoe Russell-Stretten.

Lyndsey Harris is a pseudonym. All names have been changed to protect the privacy of Lyndsey's daughter.

Betrayed

A true story of 'pure wickedness'

Lyndsey Harris with
Andrew Crofts

CENTURY · LONDON

Published by Century in 2006

3 5 7 9 10 8 6 4

First published in the United Kingdom in 2006 by Century
The Random House Group Limited
20 Vauxhall Bridge Road, London SW1V 2SA

Random House Australia (Pty) Limited
20 Alfred Street, Milsons Point, Sydney,
New South Wales 2061, Australia

Random House New Zealand Limited
18 Poland Road, Glenfield
Auckland 10, New Zealand

Random House (Pty) Limited
Isle of Houghton, Corner of Boundary Road & Carse O'Gowrie
Houghton 2198, South Africa

The Random House Group Limited Reg. No. 954009

www.randomhouse.co.uk

A CIP catalogue record for this book is available from the British Library

Papers used by Random House are natural, recyclable
products made from wood grown in sustainable forests. The manufacturing
processes conform to the environmental regulations of the country of origin

ISBN 9781846050459 (from Jan 2007)
ISBN 1846050456

Typeset in Spectrum MT by Palimpsest Book Production Limited, Polmont, Stirlingshire
Printed and bound in Great Britain by
Clays Ltd, St Ives plc

Contents

1: Big Scary Feelings 3

2: Growing Up 8

3: Forging Friendships 20

4: Having Babies 30

5: Hints of Dark Secrets 38

6: The Arrival of the Girls 48

7: The Ups and Downs 59

8: Family Friendships 67

9: Little Fire Starter 88

10: The First Signs 95

11: The Cruellest Cuts 122

12: Locks and Fears 134

13: My Bad Parenting 150

14: Secrets and Lies 163

15: Inside Sarah's Mind 176

16: The Birthday Party 182

17: Unseen Evil 199

18: Family Therapy 205

19: Keep Out of Reach . . . 209

20: A Reputation 224

21: Exploring the Dark   *243*

22: The Holiday   *253*

23: Exclusion   *265*

24: Blades   *276*

25: Letters   *287*

26: The Police Arrive   *302*

27: The Confession   *319*

28: The Aftermath   *339*

29: The Depth of the Deception   *350*

30: The Court   *358*

Epilogue   *367*

Acknowledgements   *373*

'She can both false and friendly be,
Beware! Beware!
Trust her not
She is fooling thee! Beware!'

Henry Wadsworth Longfellow

1

Big Scary Feelings

My daughter Sarah would say this is a story of 'big scary feelings' and she would be right, as she so often is. Sarah is nine now, and she was only six when all this began, but even then she could sometimes seem more grown-up than me. Children are so good at seeing straight to the point, past all the confusions and uncertainties that experience puts in your way, whereas we adults often get too wrapped up in our own worlds to see the plain truth.

I remember thinking, just before things started to go wrong, that our family life was going as well as I could have wished for. It wasn't perfect, of course:

every day would be full of all the petty frustrations and annoyances that make up normal life when you have a home, a job, a partner and two children to balance – but whose life is? And at the end of a busy day, when the children were tucked up safely in bed and I could see my husband Mike working happily away on his computer in the next room, I felt very pleased with what we had managed to achieve.

I should have known I was pushing my luck by thinking such a thing. It never pays to be smug. The fates don't like it – they see it as an open invitation to mess things up for you, just to remind you who's boss. They'll come in and turn everything upside down and make sure you know not to take anything for granted. People are always telling you to 'count your blessings', but it seems to me that if you do that too often, someone will come along and nick them.

But I didn't know that then. I thought it was fine to look over your life and decide that you'd done all right. Mike and I had been happily married for fifteen years, and we certainly got along much better than a lot of the couples I knew or heard about. The fact that he was working days and I was working nights might have had something to do with it – we didn't have time to get on each other's nerves – but even so, our placid, content relationship and the compatibility we'd maintained over the years seemed like an achievement. Most of the married couples I knew seemed to be fit to kill each other half the time but Mike and I rolled happily along, taking life as it came. Mike certainly seemed to be in a good place: happy with his job and his family and with lots of outside interests to keep him occupied.

Our greatest blessings were our two children. Luke, the eldest, and Sarah were happy, healthy, popular kids, doing well at school and making us proud. They had their less attractive moments and their fair share of real and imagined illnesses, some brought on by fretting over trivial anxieties (although not trivial to them, obviously), but they both had lots of friends and seemed to be coping well with life.

As for me, I was on an even keel, enjoying my job and my family, and taking the ups and downs of life as well as I could. I am generally happy and popular, with lots of friends. I love my work – in fact, I've loved all my jobs, even the mundane ones I had to take when I first left school. I didn't have much of a choice back then. I left early with virtually no qualifications and even less ambition. But work suited me down to the ground. I loved the social aspect of working, being around people, listening to their problems, being supportive and just having a laugh. I could never be a full-time housewife, staying at home all the time – I get bored too easily and I'm too interested in finding out how other people tick and what's going on around me.

You just never know, as you breeze through life, what sort of lives the people you bump into have led. The nice middle-aged woman who serves you at the till in the supermarket may have been hooked on glue when she was twelve; the cheerful old chap who says good morning at the bus stop could well have spent forty years in prison. It's not until you get to know people that you begin to find out what it was in the past that made them who they are today, and why they do the things they do, or think the things they think. The only problem is finding enough hours in the day to really get to know the characters whose paths I cross. For some reason, people have always been drawn to me, wanting to tell me their problems and treating me like their personal agony aunt. Everyone I meet seems happy to tell me everything about their lives, even things they wouldn't want to tell their partners. Maybe it's because I'm a pretty good listener: I find people's lives and relationships an endless source of fascination, and it just doesn't occur to me to judge them when they tell me things. I also never gossip about anyone, and people know that – it encourages them to confide in me. Or maybe it's because I don't often offer advice; I'm painfully aware that I don't usually have any answers to anything, so I just listen and sympathise and maybe make the odd suggestion if I'm asked.

Once, years ago, I had a friend whose husband was beating her up and I was doing a lot of listening to her. Just talking seemed to help, because she eventually left him and then started going out with one of the blokes at work. It was even me he came to for tips when he wanted to propose romantically to her. It was so lovely to feel that I'd made two people happy. It gave me a taste for helping people. I wonder now if that was such a good thing after all.

Looking back, now that the terrible storm is past, I don't think anyone peeking in on our cosy, unruffled family life could have predicted just how dark and dangerous everything was about to become. The horror came from nowhere, with no warning and no explanation. One moment everything seemed to make sense, and the next moment nothing did. I went from thinking I understood everything to believing I was going mad.

I was a happy, popular, easygoing wife and mother. Then, suddenly, my life was being torn apart and I was on the brink of losing everything I'd ever cared about.

2

Growing Up

I was eleven when we moved to the town where I would spend the next twenty-five years of my life. Dad had been in the army, a lance corporal in the Royal Corps of Transport, and we were continually upping sticks and going to some new base somewhere, having to settle down afresh. We even lived in Germany for a while. I think that was how I first learned to be sociable, through constantly meeting new people and starting again with new schools and new friends. It may also have contributed to my anxiety levels, and to the problems of depression that would always be lurking beneath the surface, ready to pop up and pull me under when I least expected it. Or maybe I just inherited these things from my mother, who often seemed to find life a bit of a struggle when I was little.

I was the oldest of three, with a brother two years younger than me, and a sister five years younger. When we finally settled in one place in England, Dad came out of the army and took a job as a delivery driver. Mum got lots of jobs in shops and garages, never staying in any one place for very long and never having any trouble getting work. Like me, she got bored very easily and liked a change. Mum had a lot of trouble with her health when we were kids, particularly her nerves, and even had to go into hospital at one stage. I knew she wasn't well and that she took tablets to help her cope with everything. I often had to stay off school to give her a break and to look after my brother and sister, which made me grow up more quickly than some of my friends and gave me a taste for the life waiting for me outside school.

When I did go to school, I can't say I made the most of it. I could have done a bit better in class if I hadn't got so carried away with having a laugh and messing around with boys. I certainly wasn't stupid, but I had no particular direction or ambition to keep me focused on the work. There was no great big plan to my life — some people seem to know exactly what they need to do at each stage in order to get to wherever they want, but seeing as I had no idea where I wanted to go, I could hardly create a master plan for the trip. If I gave it any thought at all, I just assumed that I would get a job, meet a nice bloke, get married and have the standard 2.4 children, as they say. As a result, I spent my time at school, like most of the others I knew, drifting along, waiting for the moment when I could get out on my own and earn a bit of money.

I always wanted to be independent and by the time I was sixteen, there were the usual sort of tensions in our house that you would expect to surround any teenager living at home. So the moment I left school, I got myself a job as a shampooist at a local hairdresser and flounced off to rent a bedsit in town. Like Mum, I could get jobs very easily but never stuck them for long – I must have inherited her short attention span along with everything else.

The bedsit was the cheapest place I could find, squashed into the attic of a big Victorian house that smelled of cabbage and damp. On my first evening there, I sat all alone, eating dry crackers and cheese. The silence was so loud, I put a Barry Manilow record on my portable record player just for company, and within two hours I realised I'd made a big mistake. A bit of family noise and friction was a great deal preferable to silence and loneliness, so I rang Mum and asked if I could go home. She was very nice about it, not rubbing my nose in it at all. My sister, however, was not best pleased, having thought she'd got the bedroom to herself at last. I've never been too good at tidying and cleaning and she'd spent all day getting the room into apple-pie order. Then I arrived back, dropped all my stuff on the floor and messed things up again.

I might sound like a happy-go-lucky type, as I drifted along, waiting for life to happen to me, but actually, like most teenagers, I was often very miserable. I think I must have inherited my mother's trouble with her nerves and spirits. It never took much to tip me into a depression, so when my first serious boyfriend finished with me and I had a row with Mum and Dad the same day, I decided there was no point in going on and I might as well end it all. Even though I hadn't really expected my boyfriend to marry me, I had accepted an engagement ring off him. Actually, he gave me his ex-girlfriend's ring and then, when we decided not to stay engaged, he asked me to go round the shops and see if I could sell it, and like a fool I did. So he was hardly Mr Right and I don't think I really believed he was, but a part of me thought that

I'd found someone who really loved me and wanted to build a life with me, and so of course I was devastated when he ended it. I was needy and insecure, desperate all the time for reassurance, and now that the relationship was over, I didn't think I would ever be good enough for anyone else.

Back home, fighting with my parents, I decided that if this was what life was going to be like, I didn't want to go on. Truly intending to put an end to my short life, I swallowed a load of Mum's tranquillisers, having secreted them in the pocket of my green cardigan, washing them down with orange juice. Then I went up to bed as if it was a normal night, without bothering to write a goodbye note or drop any hints about what I was up to. I felt absolutely no qualms or regrets or last-minute changes of mind, but just allowed myself to drift off to sleep peacefully. It was like a weight had lifted off my mind: I no longer had anything to worry about.

I was even more fed up when I woke up the next morning and realised I was still alive. Now I had a failed suicide bid to add to my list of non-achievements.

Considering how many tablets I'd taken I didn't feel too bad, so I thought that as I wasn't dead, I might as well get up and go to work as usual. At the time I had a job in the local Spar shop. It was only when I got there, and tried to talk to my fellow workers, that I realised the drugs were still having a powerful effect. I couldn't get my words out and what did come out was all slurred, as though I was drunk. The tablets must have been slow-releasing and there was no way now of getting them out of my system until they had worked their way through, so I just had to try to keep going and hope no one noticed.

I managed to get through the morning by staying out of everyone's way, and then staggered the quarter of a mile home for my lunch. Mum was in the bath when I got there so I went into the bathroom to talk to her. I lowered the lid on the toilet and sat down, but I kept sliding off on to the floor, unable to make my legs support me.

'You've been taking my tablets, haven't you?' she said accusingly as she watched me flopping about. 'How could you be so stupid?'

Then panic set in. She jumped out of the bath and called my uncle and auntie round, and they all started having a go at me for being such an idiot, which was fair enough really. They took me down to the casualty department at the hospital but by this time the drugs had been in my system for twelve hours or more, so there was no point pumping my stomach out. My heart was thumping all over the place, so they made me wear an external pacemaker for a few days, to make sure it didn't suddenly give out. They also made me talk to the hospital psychiatrist, who was convinced I must hate men in order to take such a drastic step. I didn't quite get that – after all, wasn't the problem that I was too keen? – but there didn't seem much point in arguing. Once I was out of the hospital there was no follow-up care, so I went back to coping with life as best I could, just like everyone else. I had a few other boyfriends, but no one serious for a while, which was fine by me. Most of the time I was having a pretty good laugh.

I was eighteen when I first saw Mike. I'd managed to move out of home properly by then, into another bedsit. It was similar to the first one, but this time I had a friend living upstairs, which made all the difference. It doesn't matter how basic your living accommodation is at that age if you have someone to share it with. I was young and having a good time, relishing my independence and not having to think of anyone but myself. I went out all the time, drinking and having fun and waiting to see what would happen next. Life seemed full of possibilities.

Dad and Mum used to come round to the room now and then to visit, appalled by the mess and convinced I was doing drugs, telling me I needed a good wash. However irritating I found their unasked-for advice, it was still good to know they were there for me, and cared about what happened.

Keen to have some spending money, I was holding down two jobs at the same time, one behind the bar in a pub and the other as a waitress in a pizza restaurant. I was in the pub when Mike came in with a bunch of his mates. I remember one of them putting ice down Mike's trousers and thinking the whole group of them were a bit immature, but then you see a lot of that sort of thing if you work in a pub: young blokes fooling around and showing off, trying to impress girls, and each other.

All the same, I liked the work, but I eventually got the sack from that pub for chatting to the customers too much, which seemed ludicrous to me, as I thought it was part of a barmaid's job.

At first Mike and I just became friends and went out with a group of other people a few times. Two years older than me, he was working for a hardware store, doing jobs like chopping up wood. I knew he liked me and we went out as a couple a few times. Then he became more serious about the relationship and would sit outside my bedsit, or drive past my work just to catch a glimpse of me. But the more he did that sort of thing, the less interested I became. I suppose we always want what we can't have and undervalue what's handed to us on a plate. Mum and Dad kept telling me what a nice boy Mike was and predicting I would marry him one day, which is a real turn-off for any teenager. Who wants to marry someone their parents approve of?

I started going out with one of his friends instead and Mike lost interest. Being a contrary woman, the moment that happened I suddenly became keen on him and it was his turn to keep me at arm's length for a long time. He went from one extreme to the other; one minute he told me he loved me and wanted to be with me all the time, the next he was promising he would come round and then not turning up. Or he would tell me he was too tired to go out and then I would find out he'd gone out with his friends. I started to respect him far more than when he was being the attentive lover, and made a lot more effort in the relationship, which shows how impossible we girls can be.

Eventually I realised that I was drawn to Mike because

he wanted to protect me and look after me. He didn't need me to mother him, which was the role virtually everyone else expected me to play all my life. We are complete opposites – he is very quiet, only outgoing with people he knows well, whereas I can become best friends with complete strangers at a bus stop; he is cautious, hating to do anything on the spur of the moment, whereas I love to be spontaneous – but we complemented and balanced each other out perfectly.

Most importantly, I knew he loved me, even if it was hard to persuade him to say the words again, after being rebuffed the first time. Once my eyes had been opened, I began to appreciate how sensible and reliable he was, and how right he was for me. He made me feel very secure for the first time in my life. I loved him and knew I'd be safe with him.

After another six months we were on an even keel, both of us now behaving at the same time as if we were in a steady relationship. We were a couple and everyone knew it. I even moved into his family home, having got fed up with the bedsit life by then. I was allowed to use Mike's bedroom and he was made to sleep on the couch downstairs, which didn't particularly thrill him, but Mike never complains. I got on very well with the whole family, especially Mike's brother, who was three years younger than me. We would argue just like brother and sister, which made me feel completely at home.

Mike's dad found me a bit of a challenge. Unlike Mike and his mother and brother, who are all very easygoing and allow life to wash over them, his dad had a lot of opinions and was used to being listened to. He was certainly not accustomed to being argued with, or to having someone equally opinionated in the house, so I was a bit of a surprise to him. Despite the occasional spat, however, we coped well with each other.

Eventually, Mike and I moved out of his parents' house, rented a two-bedroom house together and got engaged. It was inevitable that we would end up together: we were so well suited and so content, and living together was easy because Mike was the most relaxed person I'd ever met.

Life had become very stable. I was twenty, working at a tobacco and confectionery wholesalers supervising the telesales department. Mike was twenty-two by then and working as the manager of a tyre-changing company. There seemed no reason why we shouldn't continue on just as peacefully and happily. We got married as if it was the most obvious and natural thing in the world to do.

I had my life sorted, I thought. But the wheels of events that would turn everything upside down were about to be set in motion.

3

Forging Friendships

From my first impression of her, I would never have pre-dicted Tanya and I were eventually going to be so close and share so much in our lives. She came to work in the computing department of the tobacco wholesalers where I was a supervisor. It was 1990, I was twenty-two and she was three years older. Tanya was very quiet, always on the edge of any group, never pushing herself forward as the life and soul of any party. No one could ever say she was a beauty – she's quite masculine-looking – and some people found her stand-offish, but I liked her. A number of other new girls had joined the company at the same time, all a bit younger than Tanya and me, and there was a lot of bitchiness going on behind everyone's backs — 'so-and-so thinks you're a right cow' and that sort of thing — which didn't interest me at all. Tanya never went in for any of that either, which I appreciated, and I took to her immediately, although, to be fair, I do tend to take to most people, until they do something to make me see through them, and even then I always seem to find something about them that explains why they are the way they are. I'm often accused of being naive, and I probably am, but I don't think it's a bad way to be, overall. I wouldn't like to be cynical and always thinking the worst of everyone.

I wouldn't have guessed, though, that one day Tanya and I were going to be soulmates. It didn't seem that way at first. In fact, I hardly took any notice of her and, while I liked her, she didn't seem like the type to be a friend of mine. She was so reserved, blending into the background, and keeping herself to herself. Looking at her, I found it easy to assume that she didn't have much of a life, and no real history to share. She seemed unruffled and with no problems she wanted to confide, so I assumed everything in her life was going smoothly. She was to prove me wrong on that score pretty quickly.

A couple of weeks after she joined the company, I found Tanya sitting on the stairs one day, looking very unhappy.

'Are you all right?' I asked.

As usual, a simple show of interest opened the flood-gates and she burst into tears. 'I'm pregnant!' she sobbed.

I have to admit I was surprised; she just didn't look the type who would make a mistake like that. I knew she wasn't married and sat down beside her to find out more. All the problems and worries she must have been suppressing up till that moment came pouring out like a torrent over a broken dam. She told me the father of her baby was an abusive boyfriend who was always beating her up. It was a story I had heard often, but I hadn't thought she was the sort of person who would allow herself to be anyone's victim. So many women seem to fall for the wrong sorts of men and I guess everyone is vulnerable to bullies in some way, but she seemed to be made of tougher stuff than most.

'What do you think I should do?' she asked when she'd finished telling me the whole story.

I'm always wary of offering solutions and I didn't know what to advise her, and said so. 'But you can come and talk whenever you need to. I'm always willing to listen and be a friendly ear, don't worry about that.'

'Thanks, Lyndsey,' she said. 'You're really kind – that's just what I need.'

She seemed grateful for my offer, as people so often

are when they have something weighing on their mind but don't want to share it with anyone who might judge them. It's so easy to tell someone who is in an abusive relationship to just walk away, but it's never that easy in practice. Try telling a smoker that the solution is simple, all they have to do is stop buying cigarettes; or advise an alcoholic to start drinking water. If they were the sort of people who could just give these things up, they probably wouldn't have got addicted in the first place. Women stuck in abusive relationships always seem to be hoping that if they just hang on, things will get better and their partners will go back to being the same sweet, loving men they were when they first met them. It hardly ever happens, of course, but that doesn't stop them from hoping. Often they start to believe that it's all their fault, because that's what the abuser is telling them, and they just need someone to reassure them they're not bad people, that they're not to blame. I remembered the woman I'd helped before: eventually she found the courage to get out of her abusive relationship and find happiness. Maybe, by listening, I could help Tanya as well.

When she realised that I was happy to play the role of sympathetic listener, Tanya started coming down to the house regularly for a cuppa and a chat. It was always at my house that we had our heart-to-hearts because she was still living with her parents in the next town. She'd come over, the kettle would immediately go on, and I would still be listening three hours later if she was still talking.

Luckily for Tanya, I didn't have much else to do when I was home. I find it completely impossible to work up any enthusiasm for housework at all, which is easy to see by the state of my house. I've never been able to understand people who drive themselves mad trying to keep a family home immaculate. I would rather have a relaxed environment where everyone can do what they like without ruining the feng shui. It's not that I don't like a house to be nicely decorated and comfortable, I just think a bit of cheerful untidiness never hurt anyone. If I have a choice between wiping down my shelves and curling up on the sofa with a cup of coffee, the telephone and a couple of cats, the sofa/telephone/cat combination is always going to win. Fortunately for me, Mike is as unbothered about house-perfect as he is about everything else, so I had plenty of time to devote to Tanya's predicament.

He was also brilliant about the amount of time my new-found friend spent over at our place confiding her problems to me. A lot of husbands would have objected to the hours she passed around our house, monopolising my time, but he was never bothered. Mike was very good at wandering off at such times and amusing himself, watching television or working at the computer, apparently oblivious to whatever was being said around him. Like a lot of men, I think he has the handy trick of being able to tune out whatever he doesn't want to hear.

Tanya and I bonded over cups of tea as she opened up her heart to me. We were always together, so much so that my dad had nicknamed her 'the Shadow', because she was constantly there, lurking in the background whenever he saw me. I suppose that it must have looked a little spooky to other people, but before long I was so used to her being around she was almost like an extension of myself.

We spent long hours discussing her problems.

'Do you think I should have an abortion?' she kept asking, after she'd confessed to me that she was pregnant.

'I can't advise you on something like that,' I said. 'You can't expect anyone else to make that decision for you. Maybe you should get some professional counselling to help you understand what you really want.'

The next time I saw her she told me she'd contacted a private abortion clinic, but they too had refused to give an opinion of what she should do, as you would expect of professionals, and she was becoming more and more confused. I knew she wanted someone to tell her what to do but I was definitely not going to take responsibility for anything as serious as the life of an unborn child. All I was willing to do was listen to her as she sobbed uncontrollably, and to be there for her whenever she needed me. We went over and over the reasons why she should or shouldn't get rid of the baby. Was it fair to bring it into the world if its father was already acting violently towards its mother? Could she actually bear to end her own baby's life? Was she capable of bringing up a child on her own? Such terrible questions to have to think about. I certainly didn't feel I knew her well enough to be able to give her any answers.

I did feel sorry for her, knowing she didn't have a partner she could talk it over with, but the more I listened to her the more she talked, ringing me up at one or two in the morning when she was unable to sleep because of the anxieties and conflicts swirling around in her head. Whatever the time, I would listen because I know how it feels to be low in the middle of the night when the rest of the world is sleeping peacefully and there is nothing to distract you from the fears that rise up to haunt you.

In the end she decided to go ahead with the abortion. I could see it had been a terrible step for her to take. Once the decision was made, however, she seemed to be happier and stopped coming round to the house so much. We would still talk at work, as good friends, but the crisis had passed and things became calmer. She didn't appear to need my support and I was quite relieved to take a step back for a while.

———————

There was a guy called Andrew working in the warehouse, whom I'd known before Tanya arrived. I had a good, fun relationship with the blokes down there, giving them as much cheek as they gave me. Andrew was one of the quieter ones. He was quite tall and awkward, and seemed surprised by virtually everything that happened around him. He reminded me of a startled owl, but otherwise he appeared to have virtually no personality at all. Nevertheless, even though I had almost nothing in common with him, Andrew ended up sleeping on my sofa for a few nights after he'd fallen out with his mum – another example of how people seem to zero in on me when they have a problem. Or maybe I just rush in too fast with the listening ear and offers of support.

I was taken a bit by surprise when he and Tanya started going out together, but once I'd got used to the idea, I decided they would probably make quite a good pair. Her fast-moving mind compensated for his incredibly slow, methodical approach to life. I used to watch them together and wonder how she managed to hold in her temper and keep her patience. She would ask him to pop out to the shops for something and it would take him twenty minutes to get ready. He would start sentences and take so long getting to the end that I would have to bite my lip to stop myself from finishing them for him. There was no doubt that Tanya was the leader in this relationship, with Andrew happy to follow along behind, obeying orders. I was pleased to see that she had got herself out of the abusive relationship that had culminated in the unwanted pregnancy and hoped that she would never allow herself to play the victim again. It looked like they might both be heading for a happy ending.

They started going out in February and got married in September, with their first baby due the following February. The speed of the whole thing was a bit of a joke around the office. I wasn't invited to the wedding, since our friendship seemed to have settled down into being something much less intense by then, but I didn't mind. I was just glad that Tanya could be happy. In

Andrew, she had found the stability she wanted and now she would be able to replace her lost baby with a planned one. I was glad to think she had found some peace.

4

Having Babies

After her wedding, as the birth of her baby approached, Tanya started seeking me out again, wanting to talk. I could imagine that Andrew might not be the best person to confide in if you had a real problem, particularly if it had anything to do with babies or relationships, or, in fact, anything other than football or computers. I don't think he's unusual. Most men I know don't enjoy talking about problems, preferring to stick their heads in the sand whenever they think one might be approaching in the hope that it will pass them by. Women, on the other hand, like to give problems a good working over, even imaginary ones, looking at them from every angle, and then going over the whole thing again a few more times before coming to the conclusion that they still can't see a solution and will need to chat about it some more. Tanya, in particular, seemed to relish a good drama, and she was eager to get out of the bedsit she and Andrew shared and come round to me to talk it all over.

'I'm so frightened that I'm going to die in childbirth,' she confided during one of our chats.

'Why should you worry about that? Hardly anyone dies in childbirth these days,' I said.

Tanya gave me one of her dramatic looks. 'It's bound to happen to me though. I'm going to be the one that they don't manage to help in time!'

'I'm sure you'll be fine,' I said. 'Think of everything they can do. It's very unlikely anything will go wrong during the birth. Modern medicine is well up to delivering a healthy bouncing baby without losing the mother in the process.'

Tanya persisted though. She couldn't stop insisting that she was sure it was all going to go wrong. Even if she did harp on, I could see that it was a genuine fear and I listened, sympathised and tried to reassure her that it was going to be all right. I understood that she probably couldn't talk to Andrew about it, at least not if she was hoping for any useful sort of reaction. Even Mike, a relaxed and understanding husband, would not really have been up to debating the intricacies of childbirth and the kind of worries women experience as they approach it – and why should he, really? So it felt right that Tanya had another woman she could turn to when she got anxious.

Despite all the worries, the birth was straightforward. Tanya had a healthy boy and they named him David. She was absolutely delighted with her baby and doted on him from the moment he arrived. She gave up work in order to concentrate full-time on being a mother and regularly brought David down to my house. I guess she had a fair bit of time on her hands and when you have a small baby to look after all day, you do tend to crave adult conversation, or at least someone to complain to. There is a limit to how many hours a day you can keep gurgling and cooing at your baby, however beautiful and brilliant you might think it is, and the little thing is asleep half the time anyway.

I enjoyed Tanya's visits: she was bright, funny and chatty and kept me amused. She and Andrew had moved out of their bedsit into a proper house, but this led to more problems. Tanya often complained about Andrew – how he was always working and never at home to help her with David or the housework, even though he had to work hard to pay for everything. Both of them seemed to have become rather obsessed with money and what they could get out of every situation. It used to irritate me a bit as I was never particularly interested in self-improvement of that sort, but I just ignored it when she harped on about how much things cost and what they wanted to buy. She also complained about how hard it was looking after a baby: you'd have thought she was the first person ever to have one from the way she went on about it. I couldn't help suspecting she was playing everything up a bit. David appeared to be a very good child but to hear Tanya, you'd think he was the most time-consuming, difficult infant ever born. But most of the time, despite Tanya's tendency to moan, we had a great time together and we seemed to be able to talk for hours without even noticing the time going by. She would go home and half an hour later we would more often than not be gossiping on the phone again, as if we hadn't spoken in months.

Getting pregnant was now firmly on my agenda. The obvious next step in life after finding a nice husband and settling down in our own home was to have a baby. Although I could see from watching Tanya with David that it wasn't all plain sailing, I was beginning to feel distinctly broody. Mike and I stopped taking precautions, so that nature could take its course.

It didn't happen at once, and then I had a couple of very early miscarriages but the doctor assured me there was nothing to worry about yet and in the autumn of 1992, I discovered I was pregnant, by which time I was twenty-five years old and feeling settled in my life. Mike and I were delighted that we were going to be parents and I enjoyed the excitement of my pregnancy.

When I was seven months pregnant, I stopped work. It was New Year's Eve, and all my fellow workers threw me a party. I cried my eyes out at the thought of losing so many friends, but six weeks later the company closed down anyway and everybody lost their jobs. Once I was no longer working, Tanya would come down to see me even more regularly and I was happy to have someone to talk to who had been through the whole childbirth experience so recently. Having watched her dealing with her pregnancy and looking after little David, I had a much better idea of what to expect in the coming months. There are so many things to worry a prospective mother, and the doctors only have a limited amount of time to talk, so it is always good to have a friend who is happy to listen. Although I never became as fearful as Tanya had been, there were things that alarmed me. Scans at the hospital, for instance, showed that my baby had a very large head.

'I suppose that's not surprising,' the doctor mused as he looked at me, 'you have a large head yourself,' which seemed rather rude to me, and gave me plenty to worry about for a while. The last thing a first-time mother wants to hear is that the baby's head is going to take quite some pushing out.

On 1 March, I went into labour. At first, things were very slow. The hours ticked by and I just didn't seem to be progressing at all. They put me on a drip to try and hurry everything up but it didn't seem to do anything but make the baby stressed so the doctors decided they would have to perform an emergency Caesarean. After the endless hours of labour, with all the pain and trauma that entailed, our little boy was delivered quickly and safely in the end. We called him Luke. Mike was thrilled with his new son and at first I was euphoric, but afterwards I wasn't able to breastfeed him and I started to become severely depressed. I became convinced that the staff were all talking about me, saying I wasn't a good mother and that little Luke didn't love me and would be better off with someone he could love. Once I was out of hospital and back home, the depression began to engulf me. I withdrew from everyone, unable to see the point of getting out of bed in the morning except that I had this baby to care for and in my mind there was no one else who could do it, no matter how useless I felt I was. My moods were everywhere, though mostly down. Poor Mike would come home from work each evening not knowing whether he was going to find me laughing or crying. On my first day out of hospital I tried to cook a roast dinner for him and everything went wrong, with the meat burnt and the vegetables not cooked enough. It was a disaster and I became convinced I was a useless wife as well as a useless mother. Mike did his best to reassure me, but he was fighting a losing battle. I felt completely overwhelmed by the way our lives had transformed and utterly unable to cope with it all. I wasn't up to the job, that was obvious. There was no point in anything when I got things so wrong all the time.

Luke used to scream solidly from six to nine every night and was always being sick, possibly because, in our desperation to quieten him down, we fed him every time he cried. Nothing seemed to pacify him and my nerves became more and more stretched as the weeks went by. I was beginning to think that I had misjudged Tanya and that actually she had been underplaying the difficulties of motherhood rather than overdramatising them.

I wouldn't admit I was depressed. I always found a pretext for why I was worried or tearful, willing to grasp at any reason for why I was feeling the way I was, however flimsy or unlikely it might be. It's easy to convince your-self of anything if you try hard enough. But eventually I went to the doctor, who understood at once that I was struggling with a vast sense of bleakness and worthless-ness. He prescribed me antidepressants.

With the help of the medication, and with the gradual improvements in my mothering skills and Luke's dispo-sition, the depression started to lift and I began to feel more optimistic. Motherhood was never going to be easy but I hadn't anticipated quite how difficult looking after a baby was. Tanya helped me a lot during my depression and was a great support. But having a first baby is one of the toughest things there is and I was pleased that the hardest times were behind me. Or so I thought.

5

Hints of Dark Secrets

Tanya would always have David with her when she visited, which I sometimes found a bit of a trial. As he became more mobile, he would wreck everything he could get his hands on. Luke would be lying placidly in his bouncy chair while David went wild around him, destroying everything he could. It may have been that he was the first small child I'd had prolonged exposure to, or he might have been going through a bit of a difficult phase; either way, it was all I could do not to tell him off, even though he wasn't my child. Tanya never seemed to mind me saying no to him, but she didn't usually do anything herself to stop him, just sitting there as he ran amok around her, breaking things and eating the cat food. It would drive me mad, but I reasoned that she needed to come round to our house for a change of scene – otherwise she would have been at home with David alone all day. Young mothers need each other because no one else can stand to be around their children for long, and no one else wants to spend their whole time talking about feeding habits, sleeping routines and bowel movements. When two new mothers get together, they never have any shortage of shared interests to discuss. I was grateful to have Tanya around so that I wasn't alone all day with Luke. I could ask her things about him that were bothering me, and she gave me tips from her experience.

We spent hours walking in the park with the children, Luke in his pushchair and David racing about, diverted by everything he saw, chatting away. We talked about our childhoods and the way we had grown up. Tanya told me about her sister, whom she felt was more attractive and more successful than she was. It was obvious that this was a source of strong feelings in Tanya and gave her a deep sense of insecurity. It must be hard to believe you are in the shadow of someone else, and to feel everyone prefers that person to you, including your own parents, people who ought to love you unreservedly and without giving preference to any of their children. Tanya was sure her parents didn't love her as much as they did her sister, which must be a hard thing for anyone to live with.

'I was always the bad one in our parents' eyes,' she told me, 'and she was always the good one. I could never do anything right and she could hardly do any wrong.'

She had an older brother, but she talked less about him. Her relationship with him didn't affect her in the raw way her relationship with her sister did, and she didn't seem to have any strong feelings about him either way. It seemed that Tanya's family wasn't terribly close.

One day we were out in the park and Tanya was chattering away. I was watching David running round the edge of the pond chasing ducks so I was only half listening to her but it gradually dawned on me that she was intimating she had been abused as a child by her father. Naturally I was horrified but I didn't want to jump to the wrong conclusion or say something insensitive, so I didn't question her about it and she didn't go into any detail. Instead, she left the hint hanging in the air and I waited to see if she wanted to tell me more.

'I've been going to see my health visitor,' she said, 'at her house, to talk about my past.'

'That sounds like a good idea,' I said carefully, nodding. I'd never met this health visitor, but if Tanya had suffered in the way she was hinting, it was wise to talk to a professional. I certainly didn't feel qualified to give advice about such difficult and potentially unsettling subjects. She carried on talking but I kept my mouth shut and didn't follow up on the hints she was dropping. I was happy to listen to what she had to tell me but I didn't want to do more than that. She didn't expand on the subject and I felt it was better if she got her support and advice from people who really knew what they were talking about, so eventually our conversation drifted to other topics. But it was my first clue that the reality of Tanya's life was far from the straightforward image she presented.

As David got bigger and more active we started to go to Jungle Jim's, an activity centre for small children where they could climb and jump and fall in safety, submerging themselves in ball ponds, bouncing on inflatables and clambering around on ropes, surrounded by nets and soft landings. The idea was for them to play in a totally safe environment; the only potential danger was other children. Able to take our eyes off our charges for a few minutes in this controlled environment, Tanya and I could relax, have a cup of coffee and do what we did best: chat.

I'd noticed that Tanya was a very competitive mum. It wasn't an issue between us because Luke was a good bit younger than David, but she had a friend with a little girl the same age as David who, being a girl, was doing everything sooner and better than him. It drove Tanya mad. I never really liked this other woman. She never seemed to smile and I felt she was competing with me for Tanya's friendship.

'She thinks her daughter is so bloody fantastic,' Tanya would say furiously. 'What's wrong with David? Why isn't he developing so fast?'

'Don't worry. It's just a gender thing. Girls grow up quicker than boys, everyone knows that. David will catch up in the end, just as all boys do.' I tried to reassure her but I could see it was really getting under her skin.

Although Tanya was my friend and I was fond of her, there were aspects of her that I didn't like all that much. She was obsessed with David and wouldn't let anyone else do anything with him, not even Andrew – in fact, especially Andrew. Nothing the poor man could do for his son was ever right. Everything he said she would mock and belittle, and she would never allow him to tell David off. The only people she would trust with David were her mum, and me, and even then she would only leave him with us if she absolutely had to, rushing back the moment she could.

I could see that this wasn't an entirely healthy approach to have to your child, particularly where its father was concerned, but it wasn't my place to say anything.

David could be an odd child sometimes and I found it surprising that a boy so little could sometimes be naughty in the strangest ways. I would watch him going up to another child to give them a hug, which would set all the adults cooing approvingly about how 'sweet' he was being, because they didn't realise that he was actually squeezing with all his might. He would keep tightening his grip, while smiling up innocently at the adults, until his victim would burst into tears and look like a right killjoy.

We were at Jungle Jim's one day when David was about eighteen months old. I'd noticed him disappearing into the toilets with a determined look on his face and when he hadn't emerged after a few minutes I thought I'd better go in to find out what he was up to and see if he needed any help. The moment I opened the door I heard the screaming and found him dragging another toddler around by his hair. I separated them up and took him back outside to his mother. There was no getting away from the fact that David was not always an easy child. Even though she worshipped the ground he walked on, Tanya was quite strict with him when she did catch him being unkind, making him take 'time out' from play, or taking him home as a punishment. More often than not, however, he got away with it. I was very fond of David but I guessed that there was more going on behind his sweet smile than it appeared.

As usual, Tanya was always very dramatic about everything. She'd been the same since I first got to know her. If she stubbed her toe, she would be rolling around on the floor for ages shouting and screaming and clutching her foot. Every little thing was a disaster of epic proportions, with all the emotional outcry to go with it. It used to get right on my nerves, but at least I didn't have to live with it. It was worse for Andrew at home. If she'd had a bad day she was quite likely to throw his dinner at him when he got back just to let him know how much she was suffering. She was actually quite a good cook when she took the trouble, which wasn't often. She was very lazy, always leaving the housework to Andrew, even though he was working and she wasn't. Sometimes I thought he must have the patience of a saint, but I didn't feel too sorry for him because he never stuck up for himself or answered her back. He took it all without a word.

Whenever I felt myself getting annoyed with her, I would remember the little glimpse she had given me into her troubled childhood and realise that I had to make allowances. Tanya had always needed to get noticed when she was a child – it was no wonder she made a song and dance about everything now. I recalled the things she had hinted at that day in the park, but I didn't even want to guess at what she was trying to tell me. If what I suspected was right, then Tanya had suffered the kind of horrific childhood that most of us only read about. Thank goodness most of us think of home as a secure place where we are loved. To have that reversed, with the people who should love you best abusing you, hardly bears thinking about. You never know what is going on in other people's heads, or what damage has been done to them by things that have happened in the past. From time to time I felt a bit irritable with her, but then I reminded myself that she might have suffered in ways I could never imagine, so I never got cross enough to risk hurting her feelings or causing a split in our friendship.

When Luke was just over a year old, Mike and I moved to a house that was further into town. The move took us away from most of the friends we had built up in the early years of our marriage, but the new house, which Mike's parents very generously helped us to buy, was nearer to Tanya and Andrew, so we naturally started seeing more of each other than before, going to one another's houses for meals and sharing a lot of family occasions.

Mike and Andrew were both very easygoing men, always happy to fall in with whatever arrangements Tanya and I had made, as long as it didn't interfere with their pleasures. It's always quite hard when you have children to find families who fit into yours at every level but when we mixed with Tanya and Andrew, there was someone for everyone. He and Mike could chat about their computers and whatever else interested them, or just sit having a beer in companionable silence; David and Luke entertained each other, and Tanya and I got on with all the talking. There comes a stage when those sort of friendships are almost like extended families. You can hardly even remember how you first became friends, but you grow closer and closer with the passing years, partly through habit and partly through an increasing library of shared experiences. We did all the same things, we knew all the same places and people, we had many of the same thoughts and feelings. We had shared memories of the boys and the funny things they had said and done. We had grown together without even really noticing and had come to rely on one another a lot.

6

The Arrival of the Girls

As he grew older, David was one of those children who are keen to appear loving and giving, and so eager to please the adults around them that they can actually start to sound quite disturbing. He was the sort of child who is always telling people how much he loves them and being overly polite in order to impress with effusive pleases and thank-yous. A lot of it was down to the way Tanya had brought him up, but some seemed to stem from his own nature. He was very intuitive about when other people were upset and was always quick to offer comfort, which could be very charming, but also strange at the same time. Like his dad, he was not particularly physical and he had his mother's way with words, which sometimes got him into trouble with other children. Rather than fight with his fists, he would use his tongue, and his grown-up vocabulary could make him sound rather pompous, making the other boys want to hit him even harder. Little boys who talk like adult women do tend to get up people's noses a bit.

Luke was very different – he was more up front and less eager to please people outside the immediate family, although he did now and again tell Tanya he loved her. He was genuinely fond of her, as most children are of adults who have been in their daily lives for as long as they can remember. But Luke never liked David, even though they had been playing together for as long as he could remember. As soon as other friends started to come into his life, he drifted away from David and only really played with him when we were together as families. They didn't become enemies or anything, they were always perfectly OK with each other, but they just grew apart as the months went by.

Meanwhile, Tanya and I were growing ever closer. I found being with her very easy: we had much the same outlook on parenting and we could always find things to talk about. We were each other's therapists, always on hand to listen to the problems of daily life. If I sometimes found it a bit wearing and time-consuming to listen to all her complaints over everything, however trivial, I reminded myself that that's what friends were for, and that she listened to me when I was worried about Luke. But while she rang up to moan about Andrew and all his shortcomings, I didn't have anything to say about Mike. He and I never rowed, and our life together was calm and easygoing, just like him. He nearly always agreed with whatever I said in order to get a quiet life, or else ignored me and went his own way. It is almost impossible to pick a fight with Mike because he just never rises to the bait; nothing bothers him that much, which is a strength in many ways, but it meant I needed some-where to vent the irritations and worries of life, and that was where Tanya was a great help.

Two years after having David, Tanya fell pregnant again. Despite being terribly sick, which had never hap-pened when she was carrying David, she was very excited at the thought of another baby. Even though I had gone back to work, selling vacuum cleaners over the phone, I used to go with her to the hospital for her appoint-ments and on one occasion we took the boys in with us to see her scan. They became quite involved in the whole process, sharing the excitement of the preparations. It was touching to see.

One day Tanya and I were in my kitchen, waiting for the kettle to boil and I was feeling her belly, remarking on how hard it was becoming. When we took our tea through to the living room we found David and Luke lying on the floor feeling each other's bellies with the same serious expressions they must have seen on our faces. It's funny how little scenes like that stick in your memory.

The due date was approaching quickly and Tanya began thinking about the birth.

'Would you be my birthing partner?' Tanya asked, taking me by surprise. It had never occurred to me that women with partners would want to have someone else with them at the birth. I know that in the old days, when women gave birth at home, there would always be lots of other women around, and the men would make themselves scarce, but I thought things had changed now.

'Yes, of course,' I said, flattered by the request but worried about the responsibility. 'If that's what you'd like.'

'But you won't be offended if I change my mind and send you away halfway through, will you?' she asked anxiously.

'No, of course not,' I assured her. I remembered how fraught things could become during a labour and certainly wouldn't have taken it personally if she had decided, in a moment of intense pain, that my cheery face and banal encouragements were getting on her nerves.

As part of the build-up to the great day, she gave me a pager, so she could let me know as soon as she went into labour and I could drop everything and rush to her side. I wore it all the time but she kept setting it off while I was at work to make sure that it was working, which drove me mad.

'Stop doing that!' I exploded on about the fourth time. 'Otherwise I might not respond when it's the genuine call.'

'I was only testing it.' Even over the phone I could tell she was pouting. 'I don't want anything to go wrong on the day. I can't do this without you.'

By the time she finally went into labour – after two panic-filled false alarms – I had found that I was three months pregnant myself. It seemed our lives were always going to be running along parallel lines from now on, with me always following a few months behind her.

After much soul-searching, Tanya reluctantly agreed to allow Andrew's mum to look after David, since even she couldn't really expect the midwives to let him hang around in the delivery room, and she and I set off for the hospital. When we got there she was only two centimetres dilated. I could see a long wait stretching out ahead of us and suggested we went home to pass the time there. Tanya insisted that was out of the question, and that she was in too much pain to go anywhere. I could see she was stoking up the drama again, but if you can't be self-indulgent at a moment like that, when can you? To fill in the time, I made a few phone calls for her to let everyone know what was happening. I took particular pleasure in phoning her miserable friend with the precocious daughter and letting her know that I was the one she had chosen to go to the hospital with. I felt a bit ashamed of the little feeling of triumph I was experiencing, but didn't allow that to spoil the enjoyment of the moment. Every grown-up needs to behave like an immature child now and again, after all.

I rang Andrew at work and told him things were progressing and that he should get down to the hospital as soon as he could. I could tell from his voice that he was dithering about and wondered if perhaps he thought that me being there was going to let him off the hook. As he didn't drive he was going to have to get a lift and he was managing to make it all sound very complicated. I suppose the false alarms had made him a bit complacent about the whole thing. As I finished making the phone calls, I realised I hadn't had any lunch and was now hungry.

'Let's go over the road to the shop,' I suggested, thinking that would help to pass the time and might even speed her up a bit.

'I can't, I can't,' she protested. 'The pain's too much.'

'Don't be so silly,' I replied in my best nannyish voice, 'of course you can. It's only just across the road.'

'I can't, I can't!'

I could see she was panicking, but I was hungry and this looked like it might be about to turn into a marathon session. I couldn't be sure when I would next get a chance to eat, so I sat her down in a corner of the waiting room and nipped quickly across to the shop. By the time I came back, there was full-scale drama in progress.

'I told you,' Tanya crowed happily as they wheeled her away.

Her waters had broken and everything was now under way at top speed. She was doing very well, hardly making any fuss, although she kept saying she wanted an epidural and apologising to me as if I would think less of her for not wanting to endure unnecessary pain.

'I don't care what you have,' I assured her. 'If I was you, I'd have had one ages ago.'

By the time the consultant came in, it was too late for an epidural anyway; she was too far gone.

'Don't you leave me,' she begged the consultant, with

maximum drama, as if mere nurses and midwives couldn't be trusted with a birth as sensitive as hers, but he'd already gone to deal with another emergency. Tanya always found it quite hard to accept that she wasn't the centre of the universe at times like that. Maybe all women are the same in childbirth; having an enormous baby pushing its way out of you does rather tend to make you lose interest in anything the rest of the world might be up to.

I rang Andrew a few more times to hurry him up but he was still dithering around and in the end he missed the birth by five minutes. When he did finally arrive he told me the car he'd got a lift in had broken down, but I thought it was more likely he just didn't leave work on time. My theory is that there are a lot of men who, if they are being strictly honest, don't much like being present at their wives' labours. There's a lot of pressure on them to be 'involved' and I think quite a few of them are there because they have been made to feel guilty. I don't blame them for trying to get out of it. I found it quite hard seeing someone I loved in so much pain, but I stuck it out, holding Tanya's arms and encouraging her to push with the midwife as the head finally appeared.

The little girl popped out without too much trouble in the end and once Andrew had turned up, I took a quick picture and left to relieve Andrew's mum of David. The proud new parents called their daughter Amy.

Being a birthing partner had been a terrific experience and it bonded Tanya and me even closer. We had a new level of trust and acceptance, and I was honoured that Tanya had thought so much of me that she wanted me present at her baby's birth. I was surprised how different it had all seemed to when I was doing it myself. When you are actually giving birth, you are so internalised and concentrating so hard on your own pain that you are not really aware of half the things going on around you. I had a new respect for the fathers who have to watch their wives going through the ordeal. A few years later, I attended when my sister was giving birth and I cried nearly all the time to see her in so much agony when her epidural didn't work. We have become so used to having all our aches and pains taken away by pills and injections that it is a shock when you come up against nature in the raw like that. It hardly even hurts to go to the dentist any more but most women still have to get a baby out with virtually no pain-killing help at all.

When it came to my turn again six months later, I asked Tanya to be with me during labour but she said she couldn't because she had to look after David. Even now she had a new baby, she still didn't like trusting him to anyone else if she could avoid it, certainly not to her poor husband. So I had two other friends keeping me company through the labour, but I didn't want anyone there at the actual birth except Mike. I didn't want to have to worry about how I was looking or what I was saying when it came to the final stages.

Much to my relief, the birth went smoothly and I was overwhelmed with happiness when they first placed my baby girl in my arms. She was so tiny and helpless and beautiful, and I was filled with love and a desire to protect this little thing. Mike and I were over the moon – it felt as though our precious daughter completed our family, and we called her Sarah. Tanya was the first person I rang after the birth, and she and David were my first visitors in the hospital. Tanya held Sarah when Luke came in, so I was able to give him lots of attention and make sure he didn't feel left out. He was still only three years old and I didn't want him to think that Sarah's arrival meant I wouldn't have time for him. I asked Tanya if she would be one of Sarah's godmothers and she was thrilled. She seemed the obvious choice as she was the person Sarah was likely to see the most of, apart from her close family. Although she could be annoying at times, she had proved herself to be the most loyal and loving of friends.

Now Tanya and I each had a boy and a girl. Once again it seemed our lives were running in tandem, making the bond between us even stronger. We now shared the problems of juggling the needs of busy toddlers with the equally urgent needs of new babies, not to mention the needs of husbands and the rest of the world!

I couldn't imagine what my life would have been like without her.

7

The Ups and Downs

Both the boys were very good about their newly arrived sisters, showing no signs of insecurity or jealousy, although Luke did accidentally roll Sarah off the sofa on to a carpeted concrete floor when he was trying to be helpful by moving the furniture back after I'd hoovered. She didn't seem any the worse for the tumble and, seeing how mortified he was by her screams, and mine, I was pretty sure there hadn't been any malice intended. He seemed genuinely fond and protective of his little sister which made me very proud of him. Tanya and I were both congratulating ourselves that we must have done something right as he and David accepted so graciously the change in their status as only children.

In the early days of motherhood it's always such a relief when something goes right, since you never really know if you're doing things as you should or not. Mostly, you just follow your instincts and hope for the best.

Tanya got a little depressed after Amy was born, but I think it was more tiredness than anything. She always hated to ask for help with her children, seeing it as a sign of weakness, and ended up doing everything herself. She wasn't quite as possessive of Amy as she was of David, but she still preferred to look after her every need herself. Her mum came and stayed with her for a couple of days after Amy arrived, which she had done when David was born as well, but that was about as much as she was allowed to contribute to the proceedings.

Once I'd had Sarah, Tanya used to come over to the house a lot, so we could bath them and do all the other baby chores together. It was nice to have company if Mike wasn't around, and even when he was around he wasn't as entranced by the babies as we were. Like most fathers, his interest in the whole thing picked up steam once the children could talk and started wanting computers, bikes and trips to football matches. Until then, he was happy to leave the hard graft to me and generally do as little as he thought he could get away with.

When Tanya and I weren't together physically, we would be ringing one another with each new panic or fresh development. It's amazing how many times a day you can get anxious when you have small children. For me, there was always an underlying fear, just waiting to break out into a full-sized flap at the first sign of a rash, splutter of a cough or prolonged bout of inexplicable crying. There seemed to be so much potential for me to damage my children in so many different ways, since there appeared to be virtually no rules at all on the correct way to bring them up in a world that was stacked with dangers, from sharp objects to viruses.

Tanya usually came round to ours because I'm never very comfortable in other people's homes; I get bored too easily and fidgety and ready to leave after half an hour of sitting around in someone else's space. It's not as if I do much more when I'm at home, but I just feel more relaxed and at peace. When people come to my house, they always seem to stay five or six hours, so perhaps they find it as relaxing as I do. Tanya in particular used to stay for hours on end. Sometimes it felt a bit like she lived with us.

I had become very badly depressed during the second pregnancy, at the same time as Tanya was having some mild symptoms of post-natal depression, but I wasn't allowed to go on any antidepressants because of my condition, and this low continued after the birth, not helped by my hormones being all over the place. I found being with Tanya helped me to cope with the black moods, providing a welcome distraction as well as a ready pair of helping hands. I don't know what I would have done if I had been trapped in the house on my own, talking baby talk all day, trying to balance Luke's needs with Sarah's. Tanya and I had grown so used to one another now, we always seemed to be on the same wavelength. Gradually her friendship was becoming one of the most important things in my life.

I became dogged by black depression that filled me with despair. I'd always been prone to feeling low, and to anxiety attacks, but now I was laid flat by the extent of my misery. It was so difficult to deal with and at times I felt like a stranger to myself. At one of my lowest periods I became obsessed with the idea that Mike was having an affair with another of my friends. It was totally unreasonable since he'd never given me the slightest reason to distrust him, but I just didn't seem able to convince myself that I was being stupid. I might be able to reason it out for a while, but then I would remember that that was the sort of thing all women did, particularly those who were having the wool pulled over their eyes by treacherous husbands, and the panic would rise up inside me again.

This other woman was another person, like Tanya, who seemed to want my exclusive friendship and was at the house a lot. She was quite intense and seemed to be coming round every night. I became so fixated on this imagined affair, and so deaf to his exasperated denials, that I even started going through Mike's phone and his pockets in search of incriminating clues, something I would never have done in the past. Not surprisingly, I never found anything and Mike was remarkably patient with my delusions. Even now I feel guilty when I think about how I treated him, but it is a testament to the man that he forgave me and doesn't remind me of it. He understands that I was in the grip of something much stronger than myself and that it was not the real Lyndsey making those accusations.

Tanya was very good about listening to me and didn't fuel the fire by becoming dramatic or adding to my ludicrous suspicions, as some people might have done. Poor Mike is the least flirtatious man you could ever meet and never did anything to deserve such treatment. The more convinced I became of his infidelity the more unreasonable I was. I didn't like him going out and I kept accusing him of meeting her on the sly, but he never lost his patience. Maybe he was a bit flattered that he could still provoke such powerful feelings of jealousy in me. I suspect he was quite grateful that I had Tanya to talk to, since it saved him having to shoulder the whole burden of keeping me sane. Once my hormones settled down again, I realised how stupid I was being and I was very grateful to him for being so understanding and patient.

Tanya's relationship with Andrew, however, was not improving with time. It was usually pretty calm during the week, when he was at work and out of her way, but every weekend she would ring me in the middle of one of their rows, wanting me to referee the fight. I think most of the rowing was actually on her side, and the more he shrugged and muttered his excuses, the more infuriated she would become. Even while I was still on the phone, I would be able to hear her telling Andrew that I was agreeing with her about how terrible he was, when I was never saying any such thing. Her wrath could be stoked by something as trivial as him not emptying the kitchen bin when she asked, and she would go on and on at him, long after he had given in and done whatever it was she wanted. She'd get very cross with me if I ever dared to suggest that she might be in the wrong over anything. As far as she was concerned I was her friend and a fellow woman, so I should stick up for her whatever the situation. But I was never willing to tell her what she wanted to hear if I disagreed with her, even though it would have meant a more peaceful time for me if I had. I started to dread the phone ringing on Saturdays. This was the unreasonable Tanya, who couldn't resist playing any situation for its full dramatic potential and who let rip with the extent of her anger over things I thought were trivial. It was hard to deal with this Tanya sometimes, but I knew that she had been patient with me when I'd been in the grip of unreasoning suspicions, so I tried to rein in my feelings about this side of her character.

By the time Amy was six months old, Tanya's marriage had deteriorated so much that Andrew seemed to be on the brink of leaving her and the kids. I didn't think their marriage was going to make it, expecting Tanya to use this as an excuse to get out of a relationship that had always caused her so much annoyance and unhappiness. But she seemed instead to thrive on the drama of their arguments and played the fights to their maximum dramatic potential. Shakespeare would have been proud of some of the scenes she staged. I think Andrew even went to stay with his mum for a bit to try to get his head together. Tanya would ring me at two or three in the morning and talk on and on, pouring out her hurt and anger. I tried to be supportive, as she had been for me when I was struggling with trusting Mike.

'If you're going to make this marriage work,' I said, when things had been going on for some time and it looked like Andrew wasn't going to leave, 'you are really going to have to make an effort to stop putting him down all the time. You can't expect any man to put up with that. He is the father of your children and you must let him have something to do with them, you can't keep cutting him out.'

She was surprisingly good at taking this sort of advice. She had been a bit better at letting him do things for Amy, but she still didn't allow him anywhere near David and had a habit of belittling him in front of the boy whenever he spoke up or did anything for him.

Once they had decided to try to keep going, they went to a marriage guidance counsellor and to a family therapist, Tanya reluctantly allowing me or her mum to babysit during their sessions. Somehow they worked things through, finally settling back into the routine they had before the children came along and both of them promising to make more of an effort.

8

Family Friendships

When Sarah was about three and a half we moved again to a bigger house so that we had a little more space. This house was less than half a mile from where Tanya and Andrew lived and it was in an area I was familiar with from my own childhood, having been to the school just down the road. I wanted Luke and Sarah to go to the same school, even though our house was just outside the catchment area.

We managed to enrol Sarah in the same playgroup as Amy, which coincidentally was run by an old girlfriend of mine, and Luke was also down for the same school as David. It was nice for them to have someone they recognised there on their first days. Tanya and I would meet every day at the various school gates and most mornings we would go back to her house, as it was just round the corner, to pass the few hours until it was time to pick the girls up from playgroup.

Sarah loved it there to start with, which was a huge relief to me. It's always hard for a mother to see her child going off into a school for the first time. If they aren't happy there, and turn on the tears every morning, it can break your heart. You know you have to go through with it, but you feel like a complete brute for making them do something that is apparently making them miserable. Luke had given me a few heartbreaking moments over the years with his anxieties, although he had always settled down in the end, but Sarah didn't seem to have a care in the world.

Then one day, without any warning, everything changed and she simply refused to go, screaming and crying when I insisted. All my insecurities as a mother came bubbling back to the surface: was there something going wrong at the school? Was I a terrible mother for making her go? Or was she just winding me up because she would prefer to stay with Tanya and me in the mornings rather than deal with all the complications of her own age group?

'Amy keeps hitting me,' she told me when I started to delve a little deeper into why she had suddenly gone off the place she had loved up till then.

This news bothered me and raised another dilemma. How could I bring it up with Tanya – and should I bring it up at all? She was touchy about her children and the best bit of advice my mother-in-law had ever given me was never to fall out over kids. All too often I had seen friends quarrelling over something their child had told them about another child, and months later they would still be arguing, full of bad feeling and resentment, long after the kids had forgotten what had upset them in the first place and had become best friends again. I didn't want that to happen to us. After thinking about it for ages, wondering if it was possible that Sarah was making it up, or whether it would all just blow over if I ignored it, I decided to say something. Tanya was good about dealing with her children when it came to bad behaviour, and to my immense relief, she completely accepted that Sarah was telling the truth. She was as worried as I was about how to handle the situation without making it worse.

We both believed Sarah was telling the truth because we knew Amy could be a bit spiteful sometimes. Sarah was never a physical child, always more ready to sulk than to slap someone, but Amy was different. We decided to go to the playgroup teachers and make some enquiries to see if we could get a more accurate picture of what was happening. They were very helpful and it turned out that Amy had only hit her once, in the heat of a quarrel on the first day, but that Sarah had obviously neither forgotten nor forgiven this blow and didn't want to take any risk of it happening again. Once we knew the truth, we relaxed and I felt better about insisting that Sarah kept on attending.

Because Tanya and I were so close, I was always aware there was a danger that Amy and Sarah might become too reliant on one another to the exclusion of other friends. I knew that Amy was quite possessive and didn't like Sarah to play with other children, which made me a little uneasy that the relationship might become too exclusive. Little girls can so easily fall out with their best friends over trivial things and if that happens they need to have other people to turn to. If they were always together at home, and then stuck together at playgroup, they would never have a chance to make new friends.

For a while, Sarah continued to make every morning horrible for me, clinging to solid objects like railings or lamp-posts on the way to school, so I would have to literally prise her fingers off and drag her in, feeling like a monster, even though I was pretty sure she was making a fuss about nothing and would soon get over it once she realised I was sticking to my guns. Sometimes she cried so much she would make herself sick. The teachers tried to reassure me that she was fine once I'd gone, but they always say that, don't they? It's not that easy to switch off your maternal instincts, which are screaming at you to cuddle your child when it is distressed, not to force it to do the one thing it seems to dread. I hated making her go against her will but it seemed, on balance, to be the right thing to do. It's these sorts of decisions that make parenting such an agony sometimes.

I told the teachers that sometimes she was making herself sick and they got the wrong end of the stick, assuming I meant she was deliberately making herself vomit. I was touchier than I should have been about it all and everything became rather heated. I was relieved when Amy moved up to big school and Sarah followed a few months later, as I realised I had got myself something of a reputation at the playgroup for being outspoken. I was determined not to repeat the mistake at the next school. It's hard to know how much fuss to make with teachers; you understand that they're used to listening to parents worrying and that they know from experience that all these problems pass with time, but sometimes they're not as understanding of parental angst as they might be. I could tell they saw me as being too much of a worrier and a complainer, so I looked forward to starting afresh with a new set of teachers.

Although they were in different intakes in the big school, Amy and Sarah were still in the same year and went to the same classes. Whatever had been worrying Sarah at playgroup evaporated overnight and they were back to being best friends; Sarah no longer made any fuss at all about going in to school. Tanya and I were delighted that peace had been restored, although I would still have preferred it if there had been a bit more space between them, just so Sarah had a chance to spread her wings a little further from the cosy nest of our two families.

Amy still wanted Sarah's undivided attention all the time and didn't like her to have other friends. The teachers noticed it and Tanya and I were sometimes called into the classroom after school to talk about the problem. Tanya never got defensive of Amy and seemed to be as keen to solve the problem as I was. I was very grateful to her for that, as I would have hated to take sides between her and my daughter, but she made sure that never happened; if I was worried, so was she.

Both the girls have strong characters, and both were learning exactly how to get the other to do what they wanted through manipulation. A pretty normal little girls' relationship in many ways, I'd guess, just a bit claustrophobic. I was fairly sure they would have been friends even if Tanya and I hadn't been so close, because David and Luke never bonded in the same way just because they saw a lot of one another when they were with us.

David was another matter entirely. There was a time when I used to dread him coming round to our house, as he always seemed to instigate some sort of trouble in their road. There was one incident where he accused the girl who lived opposite of biting him. Her mother was furious and got into a terrible row with Tanya, leaving me feeling like a real piggy in the middle as they yelled back and forth at one another. I didn't want to fall out with either of them and I could see they both thought I should be supporting them. It turned out that David had actually bitten himself in order to get the girl into trouble. Tanya was so furious at him for letting her make such a fool of herself sticking up for him that she gave him a terrible hiding. I eventually had to pull her off him and tell her that enough was enough, leaving him cowering in the corner of the room, covering his face with his arms for fear of more slaps. She and David always had a very volatile relationship and sometimes her punishments seemed way out of proportion with the gravity of his crimes. If he was naughty in the weeks before Christmas, for instance, she might take away his Advent calendar for the tiniest thing, or completely destroy his room in an explosion of temper. I didn't like seeing this rage come boiling out of her, particularly when it was aimed at her children who were still very little. But it was just an aspect of her character and David had obviously inherited it too. For the most part, she was a brilliant mother and I never thought she would let her anger go too far. Anyway, it was not my place to start telling her how to run her family.

In the normal course of events, Tanya had much more patience with the children than I did, particularly the girls with all their nonsense. She would be happy to play with them for ages, long after I had got bored and plonked them in front of the telly or suggested they go upstairs and play on their own. I was fine talking to them and going out with them, I just didn't have the patience for the childish games that they would want to indulge in for hours on end.

Occasionally Tanya and I would fall out over something, but it was always trivial and would never last for very long – a bit like our daughters, really. Tanya was often quite competitive about the girls; for instance, if Sarah was doing better with her reading than Amy she would get quite grumpy and defensive, but it just used to make me laugh. I never felt the need to be competitive with either of my kids because I was completely happy that they were learning and developing at a good rate, better than I might have hoped in fact. One day the school called Tanya in to say that Amy didn't know her numbers properly.

'She does know them!' Tanya was incensed at the suggestion her child might be backward. 'At home she knows them perfectly.'

When we were back outside together, I got my chequebook out and asked Amy to read the numbers on the cheques, which she did without a single mistake. It seemed she had decided in school that day to pretend she didn't know them. Tanya was furious with her for giving the impression she was dumber than she was. I guess she thought it reflected badly on her, although I'm sure the teachers weren't being in the least bit judgemental.

By now David had grown into a lovely boy and I had become really fond of him, so I was sad to hear that he was suffering from a bit of bullying at school. Tanya was irritated, and insisted that he must be doing something to annoy the others whenever he complained about it. I used to stick up for him even though I could understand how his manner might make other children want to cut him down to size. The poor little guy was getting a hard time at school, at home and with friends out of school. I went round to their house one afternoon, when David was about eight, and he was cowering in the corner, apparently frightened of his mother.

'Get her away from me,' he pleaded. 'Get her away from me, I'm scared of her.'

I was concerned by the extent of his fear: it was upsetting to see a child so scared of its mother.

'I do get frustrated,' Tanya admitted when I asked her about it. 'It's the same way it is with Andrew. I can't help getting angry and then I explode. I know I shouldn't.'

I'd seen for myself how she could suddenly become enraged in situations that triggered her off. I felt sorry for David, or anyone who was on the receiving end of all that fury, but I never thought she would take it too far and hurt him. I knew she adored him.

'You should be supporting David if he's having trouble at school,' I told her.

'I know, I know,' she said, holding her hands up. 'You're right, you're right. I just can't help losing my temper with him.'

To give them both a break, I took David back to our house with me. The pressure of all the things that were going wrong must have been getting to him because he started acting extremely strangely. He became angry with me for no reason and began behaving stupidly, throwing things around the place, being abusive, swearing at me and calling me a 'slag' and a 'slut'. It was all the more disturbing because it was the complete opposite to the way he behaved normally, when he was so eager to please and to be loved. I didn't seem to be able to control him at all and began to panic about this little stranger who had mysteriously appeared in my home and seemed intent on causing havoc. I rang Mike.

'Can you come back home? David's started to behave really strangely and I'm very uneasy about it. I don't know if I can control him.'

'Why not call his dad?' Mike asked, not unreasonably. 'Can't Andrew deal with it?'

'There's no point talking to him,' I said. 'He's never been able to do anything with David, you know that.'

All of Andrew's authority, such as it was, had been consistently undermined by Tanya since the early days, with the result that David never took a blind bit of notice of a thing he said. Mike never says much and is quite stern with children, which gives him a sort of quiet authority that they respect, so I knew he would be able to sort it out.

'OK, I'll come back.'

When he did, we managed to calm David down eventually, but something seemed to have been released inside him. Whatever anger David had been holding in had now well and truly erupted, and over the next six months he embarked on a course of extraordinary behaviour. He began running riot around the close where Tanya and Andrew lived, throwing stones and milk bottles, smashing windows, knocking on doors and frightening old ladies, jumping out in front of cars. He also became destructive at school, jumping on tables, mimicking the teacher and generally showing off, nothing like how he had ever been in the past. He was making younger children swear, saying things like 'Your mum's a bastard!', 'Your mum's a bitch!' and 'Your mum hates you!'

I knew enough about children to understand that they repeat the things they hear often and I assumed that he was parroting the awful things he'd heard at home. When Tanya lost her temper, she would shout at him that she wished she had only ever had Amy. I dare say he'd heard a lot of the things she shouted at Andrew as well when she was angry and I knew the kind of thing that was because I'd heard it myself. Some of it made my blood run cold, like when Tanya told David she wished he hadn't been born, but even while I couldn't imagine saying such things to my own children, I tried not to judge. That was the way Tanya was, and she was at heart a loving mother. But stuff goes into kids' heads, even when you think they're not listening, and you can never be sure when or where it's going to pop back out again.

One afternoon David decided to lock Tanya out of the house. She called me over to help and I tried to reason with him through the letter box but I couldn't get any sense out of him; he just seemed so angry. I could tell that Tanya and I were both out of our depth and needed help, but I wasn't sure who to turn to. Andrew certainly couldn't have had any effect and I didn't think I could really expect Mike to start negotiating with someone else's son through a locked door. In the end I went down to the school to ask the headmaster to come up and try to get through to him, which he kindly agreed to do, although it must have seemed a very odd request.

Eventually the headmaster's air of authority and experience in dealing with angry boys won the day and he persuaded David to open the door. But that was by no means the end of the problem. He had grown a lot over the previous couple of years and Tanya and I used to have some terrible battles trying to drag him into the car to get him to school in the mornings. Even when we did manage to get him there, he was absconding all the time and Tanya was at her wits' end over what to do with him. I was so grateful that I had two quiet, untroublesome children. Although Sarah had gone through a difficult phase when she was younger, it had never been anything like this, and now both she and Luke were very obliging and cooperative most of the time.

'You're going to have to talk to social services,' I told Tanya. 'Otherwise this situation could get worse. David's out of control and I think you need professional help.'

'But they might take the kids away from me,' she protested.

Ever since David had been born, one of Tanya's biggest worries had been that the authorities would decide she wasn't a fit mother and remove her children. Even when they were tiny she had been terrified to let the health visitor know if she had made any mistakes in case she decided Tanya was an unfit mother. I could never understand why she would think that. She did lose her temper now and then, but I knew plenty of other mothers who did that, with far more regularity than Tanya, and with greater violence. No one could have doubted that she was a dedicated and concerned mother to both her children.

'Everyone needs help and advice occasionally,' I said. 'I'm sure they would admire you more for caring enough to go looking for some answers than they would if you just kept quiet and allowed things to get worse.'

I eventually managed to persuade her that they might be able to help and she made the call. That night social services sent round two family support workers. I wished wholeheartedly that I had kept my mouth shut. I was not impressed: they just stood there, doing nothing, telling us to let David have whatever he wanted. David, being nobody's fool, realised he had been handed on a plate an opportunity to behave appallingly. We ended up at one o'clock in the morning all sitting round playing dominoes with a spoilt little brat who couldn't believe his luck, loving the attention and ordering his mother to make him Mars bar sandwiches. He was even writing things on the wall like 'I hate my mum' while the social workers cautioned us to 'Let him express himself' and to 'Let him get his anger out'. All the time Andrew watched his son's increasingly bad behaviour with mournful, helpless eyes.

I had to admit that social services appeared to me to be no help whatsoever, so we continued to try to control him ourselves. After their visit, David's behaviour continued to grow worse and Tanya became increasingly tearful and withdrawn. Understandably, she relied on me more and more to be there for her to listen as she poured out her worries, but the pressure on all of us was becoming unbearable.

Around the time that David had started misbehaving, Tanya began to tell me more about the abuse she had hinted at when the boys were tiny. I spent hours over at the house talking about the problems with David, and gradually she began to reveal that she had been sexually abused by the man she ought to have trusted most in the world – her father.

'What do you think of my mum and dad?' she asked me.

'I've always thought they're great,' I answered her honestly. 'It seems as though they can't do enough for you. They drop everything, no matter what time of day or night, to come over and help out.'

I was deeply shocked to think that the truth was quite different from what I had assumed. Her parents had always seemed such nice and decent people to me. They lived above a shop and they had been round a lot to help when David was going through his difficult patch, sometimes even turning out in the middle of the night when they were needed, and taking David to stay with them for a few days to give Tanya a break. I realised that child abusers came in all shapes and sizes, but I found it really hard to imagine this gentle couple doing anything like that. I was beginning to think I must be very naive and not as good a judge of other people's characters as I had thought.

'You are so good with our Tanya,' her dad had said to me once, ruffling my hair affectionately, and I had been very touched that he was such a caring father and appreciative friend. How could I have been so easily fooled? It was incredible, I thought, that these people who had behaved in such a depraved way in their past, should be able to create such a convincing façade of being loving and normal.

'Doesn't it worry you when you let David and Amy go to your parents if your dad behaved like that towards you?' I asked, shocked to think that she would be willing to put her children in even the smallest bit of danger. If my father had done a quarter of the things she told me her father had, I certainly wouldn't be letting my children within a mile of him.

'Oh,' she said, looking startled. 'He wouldn't do it to them, would he?'

It was as if the idea had never occurred to her.

'Are you sure, Tanya? Are you really happy about David and Amy staying there?'

'Yes,' she said firmly. 'He'd never do it to them.'

I wasn't sure if I admired her for being so trusting or

not. It worried me deeply and I thought very hard about it. I was absolutely certain without a shadow of a doubt that Tanya would never do anything to harm her children, or let anyone else touch a hair of their heads. She also knew her parents better than anyone, and if she believed that her children were safe with them, then she must have very good reason for it. She would know before anyone else if something was wrong, and I trusted her judgement.

The trouble with David continued, and sometimes I would be round at Tanya and Andrew's house until two in the morning. Eventually I would convince Tanya that David had quietened down and it was safe for us all to go to bed, but I would just have got home when the phone would ring again.

'It's started all over again!' she would wail. 'Can you come back down again, please?' And I always did, because I knew that she would do the same for me if our roles were ever reversed.

When one child in a family is having problems it can be a terrible strain on the others, even if they don't show it at the time. It had to be hard for Amy when so much of her mother's time was taken up with coping with her brother. We often had her over to sleep at our house just to get some peaceful nights away from all the shouting. Not that they were all that peaceful. She and Sarah would squabble and bicker constantly; one would want the light on so the other would automatically want it off, one would want the window open so the other would want it shut. It used to drive me mad and I couldn't understand how Tanya managed to stay so patient with the pair of them when they behaved like this with her. But whenever I challenged Sarah about the way she and Amy fought, she would look at me as if I was mad and say, 'But, Mummy, Amy is my absolute best friend in the world.'

Tanya and I went to see every expert we could think of for help with David's behaviour. At one stage, on a particularly difficult night, the doctor came out and offered to sedate him, but David refused to take the tablets, which I suppose was fair enough. We even called the police in the hope they could talk some sense into him. While they were there he was very calm and reasonable, which made me suspect that he was actually choosing to behave badly in order to punish his mother in some way. I think the police were a little puzzled as to how a bunch of adults couldn't control one small boy.

'You are allowed to restrain him, you know,' they told

Andrew, but received only a baffled smile in reply.

David was always an imaginative child and his behaviour would change whenever he had been struck by a new idea. After watching the movie of *101 Dalmatians*, for instance, he started acting like Cruella de Vil, which really spooked me out, partly because he was so good at it. If anyone had ever told me I would be scared of an eight-year-old boy vamping it up as a fictional baddy, and a woman at that, I would never have believed them. Another time he threatened to take a golf club to my car and sprayed 'Fuck Off Bitch' down the side with coloured hairspray. It seemed to me we were moving into very dangerous territory indeed.

No matter how wild David became, however, he never hurt Amy, and he was always very fond of Sarah, so I never felt frightened that he would do either of them any harm. Eventually, after about six terrible months and a house move, the bad behaviour just petered out, as if he had got bored of the whole charade and had decided to go back to being the same charming child he was before it started.

Watching David go through those difficult months made me realise just what a thin line we parents walk between happy family life and chaos. If one of Tanya's children could go off the rails overnight, then there seemed no reason why the same thing couldn't happen to me. It also made me aware of what I might have put my own parents through when I was stamping about the house being a typically rebellious and moody teenager. I wasn't at all sure how well I would cope if I had to deal with such a difficult situation in my own family and I really admired the way Tanya had handled her son. The fact he had come through it so well was a credit to her patience and love.

I hoped I would never be put to the test of having to go through anything so tough. I didn't realise that much worse was approaching fast.

9

Little Fire Starter

There was a little boy living down the road from us who was getting a bit of a reputation for being a fire starter and I was concerned to discover that Luke had been hanging around with him, and that they had been playing with lighters. I really liked this boy's mum and he himself was also one of those lovable naughty children with whom it is very hard to stay cross for long. I could completely understand why Luke would want to spend time with him and I didn't want to separate them as long as I could convince myself that Luke truly understood how dangerous it was to play with fire. I've always thought that it is important to show your children that you trust them if you want them to be trustworthy.

I am the first to admit that I have a tendency to over-react whenever I think there might be something going wrong with my children, always worrying they're going to turn into delinquents if I don't nip every little mis-demeanour in the bud, and David's recent flirtation with rebellion had done nothing for my confidence. I was con-stantly on the search for signs that things might be going wrong, so when Luke admitted that he and this other boy had been messing about with fire I immediately pan-icked big time. As usual I ran around like a headless chicken trying to think who I should call for advice. I started by ringing the health visitor as I'd always got on well with her and valued her opinion.

'I know they're out of your jurisdiction,' I said, once I poured out the story, 'but what would you advise me to do?'

She suggested I ring social services but given how ineffective I'd thought them when Tanya was coping with David, I couldn't see the point of that. Then I had a brainwave and rang the local fire brigade and asked if they did training videos to teach children about the dangers of fire. They said they did and the next day two very nice firemen came out to the house to talk to Luke. They showed him the video and explained the possible repercussions of playing with fire.

The experience of seeing how quickly a fire could spread, how easily it could kill and how horrific the resulting injuries could be for survivors was shocking, even for me. It actually made me think whether I was always as careful with my cigarettes as I should have been. It never does any harm to be reminded now and then of just how cautious you need to be.

If it was shocking for me, it was even more so for Luke, who listened to the firemen with wide eyes and his mouth hanging open. I could see he was close to tears and admired his courage and dignity in such a potentially embarrassing situation. They were the sort of men that a young boy would be in awe of and I was confident he would take anything they told him very seriously indeed. I guess it was taking a sledgehammer to crack a nut, but it did have the desired effect and once they had gone he was really upset.

'I'll never do it again,' he promised me and I had no reason to doubt his word. As I told Tanya later, I could tell that he had been truly shocked and scared by what he had seen and had realised how dangerous fire was and how foolish his little friend was to take any risks at all. Phew! Problem solved, I thought, congratulating myself on being such a proactive and caring mother.

Imagine my horror a few days later, when Tanya came downstairs with a lighter she'd found on the floor in Luke's bedroom when she'd wandered in to have a look at some new stuff he'd got.

'But where did he get that from?' I asked when she showed me. 'That's not one of mine.'

'It was just lying on the floor,' she said. 'Do you think he might have more?'

'How would I know?' I squawked. 'I didn't even know he had that one.'

All my worries returning with a vengeance, I went back into the room and instigated a thorough search. Things were even worse than I thought; I found another lighter under his pillow and yet another in his sports bag. I couldn't believe it! Where were they coming from? I knew I was careless about leaving my lighters around for him to pick up if he wanted, but I was certain none of mine had gone missing and I'd never seen any of these before. He was bringing them into the house from somewhere, but where? And why? What was he using them for? If it was because he had started smoking I would surely have found the cigarettes as well, and he would only have needed one lighter for that, not three. I had to take a firm hold of myself and breathe deeply. Mustn't panic, I told myself. Must handle this like a responsible adult and parent.

I managed to stop myself hauling him out of school and tying him to a rack until he confessed. Instead, when he got back home and I'd had a chance to get control, I confronted him calmly and maturely, asking him where he'd got the lighters and what he wanted to do with them. But, to my astonishment, he denied all knowledge of them, even though he had been caught red-handed. This made me furious, because I hate it when children lie. I know they do it all the time; sometimes they can deny they have done something when they know perfectly well you saw them do it and you wonder why on earth they persist with the ridiculous denials. But this was too serious for that sort of thing. He had promised me he wouldn't do it again and now he was taking me for a fool. I absolutely had to sort this out before it got any worse.

I phoned the fire brigade again and the same firemen came back. I believed it was important he saw that he couldn't get away with this, that it was a zero-tolerance situation. The firemen were obviously a bit put out to be called back and seemed to blame me for carelessly leaving my lighters lying around for him to pick up. I could tell they weren't listening when I said they weren't my lighters, but at the same time I was aware that I did leave mine in places he could easily get to them if he wanted them. I'd never had any reason not to, as until now I had been sure both he and Sarah completely understood the danger of playing with fire, lighters and matches or whatever. Luke could tell I was angry about him denying any knowledge, so he stopped saying he knew nothing about it and just listened respectfully to what the firemen had to say. I hoped that their obvious annoyance with him would shame him into changing his ways. Once again he promised me that he had got the message and I desperately wanted to believe him. Everyone deserves a second chance and I thought he deserved a third one as well, as he had always been a thoroughly decent and trustworthy child.

At that time I was due to start a job answering telephones at night for a doctoring service, and I was anxious to ensure that Luke had got the message before I started on that as I would often be asleep during the day and unable to keep a full-time eye on him. One of the reasons I had felt it was all right to go back to work was that both my children were so sensible and mature for their ages. I hoped I hadn't misjudged them.

Although I had the odd anxiety attack, most of the time I was confident that he wasn't going to be making that mistake again. In fact, I was proud of what I'd achieved with my children and told myself that, despite my tendency to panic and overreact to things, I was making a pretty good job of being a mother, bringing up two nice, honest kids, and building up a good relationship with them.

But pride comes before a fall. And what a fall it was going to be.

10

The First Signs

Now that the children were a bit bigger and more independent, I was working weekends and a couple of nights during the week. That meant I was sleeping through much of the days and saw a bit less of everyone, including Tanya. Even Mike and I seemed to miss each other most of the time, since he was working normal day times and was asleep when I came back in from work. It wasn't the ideal family situation, but I had always been used to working odd hours and Mike and I just drifted into the habit of not seeing that much of each other.

Knowing my family was going about its happy, everyday life of work and school, mealtimes and play made me feel content, as if we had got past the first hurdle of having babies and toddlers and were now set for the next stage, as the children began to grow and express their personalities. I didn't dwell on things all that much, as you don't when life is going smoothly; I just got on with what had to be done, as everyone does.

Although I loved working and being busy, and I got on really well with my fellow workers, I was terribly anxious about the job to begin with. It seemed such a lot of responsibility for someone with no medical knowledge. What if one of the callers died because I hadn't taken down their details correctly over the phone? How would I ever live with my conscience? Sometimes I was so nervous before going in to work I would be physically sick and have an upset stomach, just like one of the kids. I would even have nightmares about it. I began to wonder if it was worth all the agony and if I shouldn't look for another job where I felt less responsible for people's lives.

I talked to everyone about my worries: Tanya, my mum, Mike and anyone else who was willing to listen. But no one could give me any answers. Although I did feel I was being a bit feeble, I decided I wasn't going to be able to cope with so much stress in the long term and eventually I decided it couldn't go on. I went in that night with the intention of handing in my notice. Before I got a chance to go in to see the boss, however, a patient rang up who said she was getting pains in her chest. She sounded anxious but not short of breath, which would indicate she was in serious trouble, so I marked her as 'urgent' but didn't call an ambulance, which was just what I had been taught to do in a case of this kind.

Unfortunately she went into cardiac arrest while waiting for the call back and nearly died. When I heard what had happened I was horrified, even though I knew I had done everything by the book. I'd been right all along — I was an accident waiting to happen and I couldn't cope with this job. But then, as I thought more about it, I realised that I had done exactly what I was meant to do, and exactly what anyone else who was employed to replace me would do in the future. I'm not medically trained. My job was to take the details efficiently and pass them on to someone who was — that was all I could do and all I was meant to do. I didn't have to take the responsibility for the world on my shoulders. In a flash, I saw that I was looking at the whole job the wrong way. It was a useful and helpful job to do, and even if now and then things would go wrong, mostly they would go right and people would be given the aid they needed. It changed my whole outlook and I said no more about handing in my notice. From that moment on I started to relax and enjoy the work.

———————

In November 2002, just after David had been through the worst of his behaviour, Tanya and Andrew moved, this time to a house that was only a hundred yards from where my parents still lived. Andrew did a very skilful job of decorating it. They were both good at doing the whole home-making bit and it all looked lovely. I thought it was wonderful, though it did make me painfully aware that Mike and I fell a bit short of their high standards when it came to housekeeping. But if our house was a bit of a shambles, at least we didn't argue all the time, and it was a peaceful, cheerful place to be.

We spent Christmas with Tanya and Andrew the year that they moved in, with the kids getting all hyper and stupid as they do at that time of year. Mike and Andrew always got on well, and Amy and Sarah were inseparable best friends again by then. Luke and David were used to one another and always got along fine without being exactly soulmates. It was a happy time.

I came to rely on Tanya a lot to help me out with the kids if I was working; she was a great help, picking them up from school and entertaining them. She had a key to the house, so she could let herself in if I was out at work, or if I was asleep and Mike was out at work. Ours had always been a mutually supportive relationship and I knew she was as happy to help me out as I was to help her. Women with small children often form these support groups among themselves, knowing that they'll be happy to return the service when someone has stepped in to help out when things are difficult. We all know how hard it is to get through the various demands of the average day. I'm not sure that the men are always quite aware of how much of a juggling act it can be, fitting schools, meals, homework, housework and all the rest into the time available when you are working outside the home as well — or even when you're not. With Tanya's help, however, I was able to cope quite reasonably and I really appreciated having her there.

It never does to become complacent when you have children. Just when you think you know exactly how they will react in any given circumstances, they do something that really surprises you. Although Luke and Sarah were both capable of being pains in the neck, like all children (and all parents as well, of course), I believed that they were both very honest, caring and loving people, who wouldn't deliberately do anything dishonest or hurtful to anyone. I was in for a nasty shock.

The following February, when Sarah was six and a half and had moved into year two at the school, she did something that was completely out of character and undermined my faith in my own judgement. Was I one of those mothers who was blind to her children's faults, only ever thinking the sun shone out of their bottoms? I had never believed so.

It all started with some Christmas Club vouchers I had bought. Some of them were left over after the usual Christmas spending spree, including a couple of blank cheques for one of the high street shops. While the kids were out at school and we were round at my house, Tanya wandered into Sarah's room to have a look at what she'd done with all her Christmas presents.

We both used to poke around one another's houses like that, sometimes having a look to see some new decorating, or to help put things away – although there was always more in that line at Tanya's house than mine. She was always very polite and avoided mentioning what chaos I lived in, but I didn't need telling, I knew. It was a contrast to Tanya's own ordered, tidy home, that was for sure, and my children's rooms generally looked like bomb sites. But I just couldn't get worked up about it.

A few minutes later she came downstairs with something in her hand. 'Did you know about these?' she asked.

She gave me the two cheques, which had been scribbled all over and ripped up.

'Where did you find those?' I asked, astonished, unable to work it out for a moment.

'They were in Sarah's wardrobe.'

I was cross at such a mindless piece of destruction but it wasn't a really big deal. Mostly, I was just puzzled why either of the kids would do such a pointless thing. Oh well, I thought, maybe they had been playing at being grown-ups, pretending to write the cheques out themselves and had then panicked when they realised they had messed them up and tried to hide the evidence. They had never done anything like that before and I couldn't see any sense in it, but it didn't seem like a particularly malicious crime.

When Luke and Sarah got home from school, I cross-examined them a bit and they both denied it. That annoyed me more than the vandalism itself.

'Well, who else would do it?' I said irritably. 'They were in your room, Sarah, in your wardrobe. Did you put them there, Luke?'

They both continued to deny it and I couldn't be sure

which of them was lying. I could see that Luke was getting very agitated because he hated confrontation of any
sort, but I couldn't work out if he was worried because
he had a guilty conscience or because he didn't want me
to start having a go at his sister. I decided that I had made
my point and I didn't think it was important enough to
make a big issue of it. They both looked so upset at being
found out, I doubted if they would ever do such a silly
thing again.

'Well, these are my things, as you well know,' I said,
in a voice that suggested this was the end of the matter,
'so in future, just leave them alone.'

Although Christmas had only just gone, I was already
starting to collect for the next year's Christmas Club. I
would collect money from Tanya and my neighbour and
her daughter, which I would then pass on to another of
my friends, who was an agent for the club. Whenever I
saw her, I would pay their money over to her with mine,
which meant that sometimes, if I hadn't seen her for a
while, the money built up a bit in the house. A few weeks
after the cheques had disappeared, I went to take whatever had accrued round to my friend, aware I hadn't
done it for a few weeks. I discovered that sixty pounds
of the money had disappeared.

As I counted and recounted, I wondered whether I'd

remembered it all wrongly. Perhaps there hadn't been as much as I'd thought. It did sometimes happen that I found I had less money than I expected. Occasionally I found I had more, but not often, sadly. But as I thought it over, I knew for sure that I was right and that the money had gone. Immediately I rang Mike, hoping that he had taken it for some emergency or other.

'Have you been helping yourself to my Christmas Club money?' I asked.

'No,' he said indignantly. 'Why would I do that?'

I knew that if it was him he would just have laughed and promised to pay me back that evening, so I immediately crossed him off my list of suspects. I felt a rising sense of panic. Now I was really worried and frightened. A large amount of money had gone and it was going to be a stretch to replace it. The last thing I needed was to have hard-earned money stolen from me. But if I'd been robbed by someone outside the family, surely they would have taken all the money, and anything else they could find in the room. I really didn't want to believe that either of my children would do such a thing, but they were the only other people living in the house. I had been so sure they would never steal, I felt physically sick as I thought about it. Worse than losing the money was the idea that my children might have taken it. If they were doing this in their own house, what else were they doing outside? My imagination started to go wild and within a few minutes I'd written them both off as hopeless delinquents and I was picturing myself visiting them in prison. I must keep calm, I told myself. Don't get things out of proportion. Just because some money was missing didn't mean they were out on the streets dealing in crack cocaine; there might be a perfectly reasonable explanation.

My mind was buzzing. How should I deal with it? What was the right thing to do? They had always been so good at knowing right from wrong; which of them was doing this? I remembered the six months when David had acted so strangely — could it be that Luke was going to go through a similar stage? But I didn't want to jump to conclusions and blame Luke when it could just as easily be Sarah — but it was so unlike her. If she wanted money she would ask for it, and she might throw a five-minute tantrum if I said no, but that was normal, wasn't it? I had no reason to think she would ever steal, especially as I nearly always gave in to her in the end anyway; she was very clever at manipulating me, or just nagging until I saw the error of my ways, or couldn't stand the water torture a moment longer.

I racked my brains for the right expert to talk to.

Despite congratulating myself on how well everything had been going, I didn't have any underlying confidence in my parenting abilities. I'd always been looking around for any guidance I could find and one tiny thing could make me panic and rush to the first person I could think of for advice.

I decided to ring Parentline to ask what would be the best way to handle the situation. A very calm lady answered the phone, listened patiently to my babbling and suggested that I needed to find out who had done it first and then decide on an appropriate course of action. In my experience, experts are very good at stating the totally bleeding obvious at times when you are absolutely unable to see it for yourself. It's quite possible that if I had just sat down with a cup of tea and done some deep breathing, I could have worked that much out for myself.

I picked the children up from school as usual, trying to pace myself and not go off like a firework display the moment I saw them.

'I want you both to go to your bedrooms when you get home,' I said, looking as stern-faced and threatening as I could manage.

'Are we in trouble?' Luke wailed, instantly sensing there were angry words looming on the horizon and unable to see any way to avoid them. 'I wish I was dead.'

They have both inherited my tendency to get anxious about everything, but Luke is always the worst. He gets terrible nervous stomach aches over anything and everything. If there was something worrying him at school like having to stand up and speak or be in a play, he would insist that he couldn't go, even though he was really good at it when he finally plucked up the courage, or was bullied into it by me. He genuinely did feel ill in these situations, although he would always have recovered in time to go out and play with his friends after school, which suggested it was more to do with the mind than the body.

I suspect the teachers thought I was too gullible with both my children, and that I should make them just get on with things more than I did. But I knew how they felt from my own experience and I hadn't the heart sometimes to force them to do things which terrified them so much. I did have my own boundaries, however. One time Luke wanted to get out of a play and told the teacher he couldn't come in because he was going on holiday. When I found out I could understand why he'd done it, but I gave him a real dressing down for lying. Telling untruths is something I am never soft about.

As the years passed, school had made a big difference to Luke's confidence and I was very grateful to them for that, knowing that all the battles in the early days to help him overcome his nerves enough to go and participate had been worthwhile in the long run.

I made Luke and Sarah stay in their rooms for fifteen minutes to think about things, hoping that would soften the culprit up for a quick confession, not wanting the innocent one to have to suffer any longer than necessary, and then I called them down and asked them about the missing money. Both children looked bewildered, as though they didn't have a clue what I was talking about.

'Well?' I asked. 'What have you got to say?'

They looked at each other, both blank-faced and puzzled. Neither said a word.

'Come on. Stealing is very bad, you know that. One of you must have taken the money, no one else could have done it. Which one is it?'

I waited. I desperately wanted one of them to make it right by confessing so we could put all this behind us. Luke looked sick and white-faced. He hates confrontation so much, just the suggestion of it can make him ill. Sarah glanced across at him and then said decisively, 'I did it.'

A wave of relief spread over Luke's little face, replaced

by a wariness as he braced himself for the explosion from me.

'Why did you take it?' I asked, surprised that I had managed to get the confession out so easily, and impressed with her courage at facing up to the consequences of her crime.

'Don't know.' She shrugged, looking at the floor and pouting as if she might be about to cry.

'What have you done with it?' I asked.

'Don't know,' she said again.

'Well, have you spent it?' I asked, annoyed that having made such a good start she was now going to make things drawn out and difficult. She couldn't imagine I was just going to let her keep her ill-gotten gains, could she? 'What have you bought?'

She just shrugged her shoulders.

'So where is it now?' I persisted.

Another shrug and still no eye contact.

I was getting so frustrated with her lack of cooperation, I started shouting and screaming, hoping to shock the information out of her, but she just kept stonewalling me with 'Don't know'.

Luke, anxious to be away from the conflict zone, scurried outside to look for his friends.

I was just so shocked that I had misjudged Sarah. How

could I have been so wrong about her? Didn't I know my own daughter at all?

'What is it you wanted to buy so much you stole the Christmas money?' I asked. 'Are you being bullied at school? Is that it? Are other kids demanding money off you?'

No matter how many questions I fired at her, or solutions I offered, I just got 'Don't know' back.

The next day Tanya came round and I poured my heart out. She was as puzzled as I was. She had known Sarah since the day she was born and didn't have the disadvantage of wearing maternal rose-tinted spectacles.

'I would never have had her down as a thief,' she said, shaking her head sadly. 'She's such a lovely girl. And what could she be doing with the money that is so terrible she won't even own up to it?'

'I really don't know what I should do with her,' I said. 'Obviously I have to teach her that it's wrong to steal, but unless I know why she did it, how can I be sure it won't happen again? Apart from anything else, I could do with that sixty quid back.'

'Perhaps we had better go through her room,' Tanya suggested.

I hated the thought of invading her private domain like that, but Sarah had confessed to taking the money and as long as she refused to tell me where it was she had forfeited the right to any privacy. We went upstairs and started searching. It didn't take long before Tanya spotted a ripped up twenty-pound note in the corner of the room. I was quite glad to get some of the money back at least, and got Mike to tape it together that evening. We searched a bit further, but I became discouraged, partly because Sarah's room was such a mess I couldn't face sorting through it. Since I am an untidy person myself, I can hardly demand that the children do any better. The result is we do run a bit of a chaotic house. The thought of trying to find the other hidden notes was too daunting and I didn't feel I had the time to dedicate to it.

The discovery of the ripped-up note was puzzling. Why would she have done that? If she was trying to hide the evidence, surely she wouldn't have just dropped it on the floor. There were any number of places she could have disposed of it – just flushing it down the toilet would have worked. The only thing I could think of was that she had wanted us to find it, and that perhaps this was some kind of cry for attention. If that was the case, where were the other forty pounds? Why hadn't she ripped the whole lot up? It seemed to me there must be something worrying her deeply to make her act so out of character.

I made a conscious decision to stop nagging her to tell me why she had done it, hoping that it would turn out to be a one-off aberration and that, in years to come, when all possibility of punishment was past, she might explain what had gone through her mind. Life settled back down to normal and I told myself it must just have been a funny little phase; Sarah had made a mistake and now realised the error of her ways. It was all part of the growing-and-learning process.

I was working nights over the children's half-term a few weeks later and Tanya offered to have Sarah at her house while I got some sleep. I accepted gratefully and managed to get a few hours before waking up to get ready for work, just as the kids came back. I went down-stairs and found Tanya waiting for me in the kitchen, and at once I could see she had something on her mind that she wanted to talk about.

'I'm really sorry to have to say this,' she said to me as the kids milled around, 'but I caught Sarah trying to steal some of Amy's things. As soon as I went to pick up her bag she went mental, so I had a look inside and it was full of Amy's play make-up and hair stuff.'

'She didn't do it,' Amy protested loyally, not wanting to believe her best friend would do such a thing.

'Don't try to protect her, Amy,' Tanya warned firmly

but kindly. 'Stealing is serious. I found the bag and I saw what was in there, so there is no point in her denying it.'

If it hadn't been for finding the money in Sarah's room, I would have assumed that this new episode was just a game the girls had been playing which Sarah had misunderstood in some way; maybe they had been playing shops, or burglars, or maybe she had thought Amy had given her the stuff. But I had been so shocked by the theft of the money that I no longer trusted my judgement. These acts were completely alien to everything I believed about my children and I wasn't sure if I could now defend Sarah as blindly as her friend was willing to do. Apart from anything else, it was embarrassing to think that Tanya had taken Sarah out of the kindness of her heart and this was how she was repaid.

'Sarah! Why was Amy's stuff in your bag?' I shouted, angry and ashamed.

'I don't know, I don't know,' was all she kept saying, her voice high-pitched and close to hysteria. It made me even more annoyed that she thought I was so stupid she didn't even have to make up some cover story for me.

'Why would you do this after Tanya was so kind and took you out?' I persisted, trying to make my tone more reasonable, as if this was a puzzle we needed to solve together as family.

'Don't know.'

I was at a complete loss. Tanya was very nice about it.

'Look, no harm's been done. I found the things before Sarah even got it out of the house. Let's just forget about it.'

But that wasn't really the point. My little girl, who I thought had such solid moral values, was turning into a thief, stealing from her mother and her best friend. I went to work that night with my head buzzing with a mixture of anger, disappointment and confusion. I wanted to nip all this in the bud as soon as possible but I had no idea of the right way to go about it.

Tanya was very supportive and came round the next day.

'You can talk about it with me, you know that,' she said comfortingly, so I poured out my worries and the fact that I was stumped about what to do.

'It's obviously upsetting you. I think it would help if you knew the extent of the problem. It's probably just a one-off but then again . . . Why don't we go up to Sarah's room and look around, see if we can find any clues about what else she might have been up to?'

'I don't like to. It doesn't feel right.'

'I honestly think it would help.'

'Well, if you think so . . . all right then,' I said reluctantly. I was so ashamed of Sarah's behaviour and willing to do anything that might help me understand her. I felt foolish that I had ever believed my children were somehow inherently honest, and grateful to Tanya for her sympathetic advice.

The room was a tip as usual, but we set to work with heavy hearts. Riffling through Sarah's wardrobe, Tanya found Amy's wallet, with a brand new ten-pound note tucked inside it.

'She must have taken it with the other stuff,' she said, 'and I missed it.'

'Oh, God,' I moaned, looking at it with horror. 'I'm so sorry! I just can't believe it! This is terrible. I'm sorry, Tanya. I'll talk to her about it tonight.'

That evening I confronted Sarah again.

'We found Amy's wallet in your wardrobe,' I said sternly, trying to show her how disappointed I was in her. 'You stole it, didn't you? When you took her make-up, you also took her money. Don't you know how wicked and bad that is? Haven't I taught you right from wrong?'

'I didn't take it,' Sarah insisted.

'But we found it in your wardrobe. Who else could have put it there but you?'

'I don't know.'

Round and round we went in circles. She denied taking the wallet and went back to repeating 'I don't know' in response to every question. Poor Luke looked like he just wanted to crawl into a corner and die. The more Sarah and I shouted at each other, the paler and more unhappy he became. Mike was just as puzzled as me; neither of us could understand how our obliging, well-behaved little daughter had transformed into a thief.

Now that we knew Sarah was capable of stealing – taking money and hiding it on two occasions – it seemed that harsher measures would be called for. Tanya and I often searched her room, though I felt like some horrible prison officer as we did it, and nearly every time Tanya would find something else in the chaos that belonged to Amy – a ring, a hairslide or something like that. On another search, she looked in the bin and spotted her membership card for the local theme park. My horror at the discovery was tinged with relief that Sarah hadn't damaged it, as I wasn't sure I would have been able to afford to replace it. Tanya probably would have told me that there was no need, but I knew these things were expensive and I would have felt terrible.

Tanya was so much better at finding stuff than I was that I felt embarrassed, worried that she might think I was deliberately ignoring things just because I didn't want to believe that my daughter was guilty. As Tanya discovered more and more of Amy's possessions, I wondered if perhaps I had a mental block and was deliberately not seeing things in some way because I didn't want to accept what was really happening.

Then it became apparent stealing wasn't the only problem. We found Amy's homework book in Sarah's room and it was all ripped up; then we found her reading record and schoolbooks, all ripped in the same way. The girls' lockers and book trays were next to each other in school so it was easy for Sarah to get hold of Amy's things. I remembered how Sarah had complained about Amy hitting her all the time when she first went to playgroup and I wondered if she had been harbouring a grudge all these years later, half of her wanting to be Amy's friend while the other half plotted a campaign of revenge that she had only just put into effect. I couldn't understand why she had never said anything about her feelings towards Amy that would make this sort of behaviour understandable. It had been years since the first incident in the playgroup and I was pretty sure that Sarah wouldn't even be able to remember it by now. So what could have happened since then to make her behave so vindictively?

Tanya was wonderfully understanding, and her attitude seemed to be rubbing off on Amy, who remained friends with Sarah, although she was obviously upset that the person she had thought was her best friend was wrecking all her work.

For me, the worst thing was that Sarah kept on denying everything, insisting that she wasn't a thief, that she loved Amy and would never want to do anything to upset her, even when the evidence was becoming so overwhelming.

'If you aren't a thief,' I said, 'why did you steal that Christmas Club money?'

'I didn't,' she snapped, and then cast her eyes to the floor as if realising she had been caught out.

'But you told me you did,' I said, completely confused. 'Why would you try to deny it now?'

Her eyes remained fixed on the ground, as if she was scared that they might give some secret away.

'Are you saying Luke stole the money?'

'I don't know!' She wailed the familiar words and I felt frustrated, seeing her digging a deeper and deeper hole for herself. I was getting so confused. Why would she say she had taken the money one moment and then deny it? If she could just come clean and admit what she had done, we could set about putting things right and finding out why she was doing it. As long as she went on playing these silly mind games, there was little I could do to help her.

I went into the school to try to find out if they had any clues why Sarah should be behaving so strangely. Although I hated having to talk about her to other people when it was something so negative, I knew that teachers sometimes could take a more objective view of children than their parents could, and hoped they would give me some new insight into the way children's minds worked.

'Does it seem in character for Sarah to do things like this?' I asked.

'No,' they assured me. 'We're very surprised. She's always been very honest and straightforward. But sometimes children go through phases if there is something worrying them.'

'Is she being bullied?' I asked. 'Is everything OK with the other children? She won't tell me anything.'

'As far as we know everything is fine,' they said. 'She seems perfectly happy at school, at least as far as we can see. Sometimes there are things going on below the surface.'

The teachers were very helpful, taking the time to talk to Sarah on her own to try and find out if there was anything going on that they should know about, but they got no nearer the answers than I did. They told her off quite strongly when she admitted to doing some things, and then became frustrated when she would do no more than shrug her shoulders in answer to their questions about why she felt so angry with Amy. She had stopped even bothering to deny her crimes. Whenever anyone suggested a possible reason for why she was behaving so badly, like resenting me going back to work, she would grasp it, often a bit too eagerly to be believable, but would deny it later when I questioned her more closely. There was no consistency to anything she said, nothing any of us could grasp and make sense of.

'I don't know why I'm doing it, Mummy,' she would say, and part of me believed her. But didn't that suggest she was even more deeply troubled than we thought if she couldn't even understand her own actions?

I was beginning to get very worried by now, and Tanya was brilliant at listening as I poured everything out to her for hours on end, the kettle constantly put on for another brew. Over the years we had grown so used to telling one another all our problems, knowing the other would never be judgemental and would always be willing to give as much listening time as we needed. She never gave me the slightest hint that she was becoming bored or exasperated as I went over and over the same territory, like a dog worrying an old bone in the hope of finding some last tiny fleck of flavour.

'Maybe she is angry about me going back to work,' I said, 'and just doesn't realise it. You know how sometimes when people are upset they take things out on the ones they love. Sarah loves you and Amy, so maybe she's punishing you because she's angry with me.'

'You mustn't blame yourself,' Tanya assured me. 'You're a great mother. You couldn't have done more for these kids. You really don't deserve this at all.'

'You are such a good friend,' I kept telling her. 'I don't know if I would be being so understanding if it was Amy doing these things to Sarah. I certainly wouldn't be letting Amy anywhere near my house if she was behaving like this.'

'Oh, Sarah can always come to play at our house,' Tanya promised me. 'What sort of friend would I be to both of you if I deserted you just when you needed help the most? I'll watch her whenever she's at the house. I want to find a way to help her as much as you do.'

I was so grateful to her. It would have been a lonely battle if I hadn't had her to talk to and share my problems. I could see that the subject was driving Mike mad and it got to the point where he couldn't bear to keep going round and round in circles and never reaching any conclusions. He stopped talking about it with me in the end – the frustration was too much.

11

The Cruellest Cuts

A couple of weeks later Sarah called me into her room. She sounded puzzled.

'Mum,' she said, 'my curtains have got a big hole in them.'

She showed me a jagged tear, which looked as if the material had got caught on something and ripped when one of us went to draw them. I looked around for a nail or anything else that could have done the damage, but I couldn't see anything.

'That's odd,' I said. 'I wonder how that happened.'

I wasn't all that interested, to be honest, and it certainly didn't occur to me to tell her off as I couldn't see what had happened. It could just as easily have been done when I opened her curtains in the morning as when she did anything.

I rang Tanya for a bit of a chat later, and mentioned the hole the curtains, just in passing. We always shared the littlest events of the day, or even the hour, things that happened to be on our minds at the moment the phone rang.

A quarter of an hour after hanging up, as I was getting on with some chores, or maybe making a cup of tea, Tanya rang me back.

'Oh my God, I'm really sorry, Lyndsey,' she said in the dramatic voice she often used, which sometimes annoyed me, especially when it turned out that whatever she had to tell me was a lot less dramatic than she was making it sound. 'I've just been into Amy's room and there are slashes all over her curtains.'

I felt a creepy sensation of sickness in my stomach. 'Well,' I said quickly, immediately feeling defensive, 'that can't have been anything to do with Sarah, can it?' I struggled to keep my tone cheerful. 'I mean, how could she have got up there without you knowing about it?'

'I don't like to have to say this,' Tanya said and my heart sank before I'd even heard what it was she didn't like to say, 'but I did find some scissors in the room after the last time Sarah was up there. I didn't think anything of it at the time, but now I've seen the slashes – well, it makes sense.'

With a heavy heart, I went to look for Sarah.

'Sarah,' I said brightly, 'Tanya's found that Amy's curtains have been cut with some scissors. Do you know anything about it?'

'I don't know,' she said, adding a bit too quickly, 'I didn't do it. I don't know anything about it.'

Did I see a guilty look in her eyes? Or was she just being defensive because she knew she was going to be the one we would all blame? I wasn't sure. I tried to keep my voice level and my rising anger under control.

'But Tanya saw the scissors after you'd been up there,' I persisted, knowing that she just wanted me to shut up. 'How did they get there? Why would you have taken them up there? What were you doing with them?'

'I don't know.' She shrugged. 'It's nothing to do with me.'

The more she refused to discuss her crimes, let alone admit them, the angrier and more helpless I felt. How could I help her if she didn't give me some clue what was wrong? What would she do next if we weren't able to address whatever the underlying problem was now?

The last question was soon answered, repeatedly.

From one hole in Sarah's bedroom curtains, it suddenly seemed they were all under attack. Every day I would find new cuts. I had spent out a lot of money on some full-length, lined curtains for the sitting room, and discovered they were covered in cuts from some sort of blade. They weren't big, dramatic slashes, just little nicks, almost invisible until you saw that the fabric had been sliced by something sharp in hundreds of different places.

Then the kitchen curtains received the same treatment, and on through the house. In the end, every pair of curtains we owned had these gashes in them, apart from the ones in my bedroom.

Once again, Tanya was incredibly supportive and much better at spotting the damage than I was. I think perhaps I didn't really want to admit that it was happening half the time, and so I wouldn't go looking for those horrible little cuts. Tanya didn't feel any such reservation and would go about, holding the curtains up to the window and showing me how the little gashes let the light through. It was easier for her, as it wasn't her daughter who was turning into a pint-sized Sweeney Todd. When she came round, she would wander through the house looking for anything that I might have missed, and nearly always found something. I rather wished she wouldn't – what I didn't know about wouldn't upset me.

Inside, though, I knew there was no point pretending this wasn't happening, and eventually I would find the damage whether Tanya pointed it out or not. We had a serious problem and I had to face up to it. Luke's curtains were the worst, and his quilt cover was slashed as well. Then my pillowcase was sliced.

All the people Sarah professed to love the most seemed to be the prime targets for her vindictive campaign. Why wasn't all this destructive behaviour being directed towards some school bully, or even some teacher she felt was being unfair to her? At least that would make some sort of sense. Why did she want to hurt people like Amy and Luke, who meant everything to her?

I wasn't nearly as bothered about the curtains as I was about what must be going on in Sarah's mind. Usually when your children are ill you know what you have to do: you put them to bed or you go to the doctor; you give them fluids or tablets or creams. There is nearly always something you can do to make yourself feel you are doing your maternal duty and looking after your baby. But Sarah wouldn't let me help her. It was almost as if she was pushing me away by pretending she didn't know what she was doing.

The questions were going round and round in my head, twenty-four hours a day. I went to sleep worrying about her and woke up with a sick feeling in my stomach before remembering what it was that was on my mind. In between, I had nightmares in which everyone was telling me it was my fault, and I knew they were right. What was driving my daughter to be so destructive? Was she seeking attention? Was she punishing me for something? Was she actually losing her mind? Was I missing some really obvious clue?

But still she refused to give any explanation.

'Don't know, don't know,' was all she ever said under questioning.

It drove Mike mad, so he stopped broaching the subject altogether and left all the talk to me. I think he was afraid he would lose his temper if he started trying to deal with her himself. Instead, he concentrated on the practical aspects of the problem. We needed to stop her gaining access to the tools she was using in her rampage of destruction, so Mike fitted locks to the cupboards where we kept sharp implements like knives and scissors. Everything we could think of was packed away out of sight and out of reach. It's amazing how many things there are around the average family house that could be used to rip material if you were determined enough. The place began to feel like a maximum security prison. How long, I wondered ironically, before we had to start searching cakes when they came into the house in case they contained files?

Because she was so good at covering her tracks and never getting caught, I began to realise that Sarah must be far more devious and cunning than I had ever imagined. I wondered in the darkest moments of the night if she would stop slashing curtains and start lashing out at people, us, the ones she seemed to love and hate in equal measure.

One early morning when it was still dark, I woke up in bed with a start, to find Sarah standing over me, just staring. Before I could control myself, before I could tell myself that this was just my six-year-old daughter who had never acted towards me in any other than a caring way, I felt a shiver of fear run through me. I strained my eyes to try to see if she had a knife or a pair of scissors in her hand.

'Can I come into bed with you?' she asked, just as she often had in the past, and I felt terrible for being frightened of my own child, a child who had always been so open and loving towards me.

How could she possibly want to turn us all against her, even subconsciously? Was that the point of the whole thing? It made my head hurt to try to make sense of it all.

'Get your cover and sleep on the floor,' I whispered, not wanting to wake Mike, who had to get to work in the morning. 'You know I can't sleep with you between me and Daddy.'

She padded back to her room to fetch her quilt and seemed quite happy to be tucked down on the floor beside us. I lay staring down at her in the dark, listening to her steady breathing as she fell back to sleep. I wondered if maybe she was beginning to frighten herself a little with her bizarre behaviour and was looking for some sort of reassurance from being close to us. Perhaps she thought she would be more able to control the demons that were making her behave so badly if we were there. That was our job, I told myself, to protect her from herself as much as from other people. We mustn't let her down when she most needed us. But what should we do? How could we be sure that whatever we decided on didn't just make the situation worse?

It wasn't like this every hour of every day. Even in the midst of all this drama, we still had space for the normal mother/daughter rows that everyone has, when we would forget about the strange stuff and just get on with daily life.

'Can I have a bra?' she asked one day, as if it was the most normal thing in the world.

'You're six years old!' I exclaimed, trying not to laugh. 'You don't need a bra. There's plenty of time for that.'

She kept trying for a bit, telling me I was the only mother in the whole world who didn't let her daughter have a bra, how all her friends had them, how I was old-fashioned and just didn't get it. I was quite relieved to be able to have an everyday conversation with her, even if it was a minor row. I was confident that my reaction was what any normal parent would have to this, and I was happy to stand my ground.

Later, once Sarah was safely at school, having apparently forgotten all about our dispute, I told Tanya about it and we both laughed. Amy had made a similar request and we could both remember the first times we had wanted to wear bras ourselves.

'I'm pretty sure I was more than six,' I said. 'In fact, I think I might have been at least twelve.'

'Times change,' Tanya laughed. 'They've got lots of things we never had at their ages.'

Maybe that was the problem, I thought, maybe we are just giving them too much, allowing them to grow up before they are ready and it is confusing them. Perhaps David had gone through his wild phase because he couldn't work out what was expected of him: was he a boy or a young man? Where should his boundaries be?

Could it be something like that troubling Sarah?

Two days later I discovered that one of my bras had been slashed in the same way as the curtains. That felt like a very personal attack. I felt hurt and a little threatened. As always, Sarah pretended to know nothing about it, although she could hardly deny it when we both remembered the conversation we'd had about bras just a few days before, and we both knew how angry she had been at being refused. It seemed like the neatest possible act of revenge, and all the more chilling for that. This wasn't simply a mindless piece of vandalism, this had been thought through and planned to make her point.

A few nights later I was going for an evening out with Tanya and some other girlfriends, and Sarah was cross with me for leaving her, as children sometimes are. They know it's ridiculous to think they could come too, but they still decide to take their resentment out on you. I didn't take much notice, giving her a kiss and a cuddle as I set off, relieved to be having a few hours when I could leave Mike in charge and forget about the troubles at home. I needed a break and to have fun.

'Forget about everything,' Tanya advised when I told her how Sarah had behaved. 'You need a laugh and a change of scene.'

I took her advice and didn't think anything more

about it until two days later, when I found the top that I'd been wearing when I went out. It had a nasty slash in it, too big and too obviously deliberate for me to be able to ignore.

There was still part of me that didn't want to believe that it was Sarah doing these things, but with each new incident the truth seemed more and more unavoidable. Why would anyone else have chosen that top to attack?

It seemed that whenever Sarah was upset in any way, she would take some terrible, secret revenge. I couldn't understand what could have happened to change a child who had previously always been so eager to please and so sensitive to the needs of others into this vengeful monster. She had always hated seeing me upset, especially if it was because of something she had said or done, but now she was acting as if she didn't care about anything, as if she actually wanted to hurt me. I began to fear that there might be something going wrong in her mind at a deeper level than I had at first thought. Where could all this lead?

I imagined scenarios of what might lie down the line if Sarah wasn't helped. What would happen if someone really upset her? Supposing, in a few years, she got a boyfriend and he dumped her, or one of her girlfriends stole him from her? What sort of revenge would she exact for that, if she was willing to avenge something as trivial as me not buying her a bra or going for a night out? Could Sarah become someone truly dangerous? It didn't bear thinking about, but I still did, all the time. My mind refused to rest, my imagination conjuring up ever more horrible circumstances.

Despite what I was imagining, I wasn't able to foresee quite how terrible things would become.

12

Locks and Fears

Nothing, it seemed, was safe from Sarah as her thirst for destruction increased. All of our clothes were subject to attack with blades or sharp objects. Toys and games were wrecked and destroyed. Luke's beloved mobile phone was smashed, the remains left brazenly for us to discover. I felt so sorry for him when he found it, as he tried to be brave and suppress his anger, and understand why his beloved sister would want to do such an unkind thing to him. Mike and I were attempting to replace his things as and when they got broken, as it didn't seem fair he should suffer, but it was becoming increasingly difficult as the damage became more and more expensive.

Both Luke and Sarah used to go to karate lessons. Tanya was with me downstairs when Sarah came running down in tears, holding her karate outfit up for me to look.

'Mummy, Mummy,' she cried, 'my karate outfit has been slashed!'

'She's a clever little actress, isn't she?' Tanya said admiringly. 'You'd never imagine from that performance that she'd done it herself, would you?'

I had to agree. Sarah, it seemed, was a very skilful little actress. Unless, of course, she truly was unaware that she was doing all these things, in which case she was a very sick little girl indeed. I wasn't sure which was the worse option. Sick might have been preferable if it was an illness we thought we could cure, but how could we when we had no idea what it was? I wondered if she had some sort of split personality, and if the normal little girl knew nothing about the things that this demon inside her was making her do when no one was around. Her tears and distress seemed so genuine, I felt like I was being torn in two. It was quite possible that she did as well.

I tried to keep control of myself and a check on my imagination. In the middle of the night, it was easy to imagine the worst kind of things going on, from the chilling to the supernatural. Was I allowing myself to be sucked into the drama of it all, having watched too many films as a teenager about children possessed by the devil? What was happening to us seemed like something from *The Omen* or *The Exorcist* – but worse, because it was so real. Once the lights came on in the cinema, or the next programme started on the television, you could put your fears behind you, have a chuckle at your own foolishness for allowing yourself to believe the fantasy, and then get on with your life. But when it was real and you never knew when the awfulness was going to strike next, or where, it was far more unsettling, and I truly was beginning to feel that there was something evil in the house. I didn't want to think that Sarah was the evil thing, but as the days went on, it was hard to see how else all this could be happening.

Then Luke discovered his karate outfit had been slashed as well and I felt myself growing angry again at the sheer destructiveness. Was I now going to have to buy him a new outfit, or make him go to his classes with a torn one? Maybe I could make some sort of repair, but I wasn't very good at that sort of thing. I felt so useless and helpless and out of my depth.

'Why?' was all I kept saying to her, even when I knew exactly what her answers would be. 'Why are you doing these things?'

'I don't know, I don't know!' was all she ever said. I wanted to believe her and as it went on, it really did seem that she *didn't* know.

I was asking every expert I could think of for their opinions, and a lot of other people besides. I rang the school nurse to see if she had any ideas what might be going on. I was desperate to find someone who would say they'd come across this sort of behaviour before and knew what to do about it. The nurse very sweetly agreed to pop round to the house for a chat.

'Is it possible she's jealous of Luke?' she asked, once we were settled down with cups of tea.

'I don't think so – I've never been aware of anything like that,' I said, racking my brains. 'I'm sure I would have noticed if she resented him in any way. They do argue, just like any other brother and sister, but she has never given me any reason to think she believes he's our favourite or anything like that. He doesn't get any more attention than she does. Overall, they're always very supportive and protective of one another. Always have been. They often say how much they love each other.'

'What about your job?' She tried another already well-trodden track. 'Might she be upset about you working? Children do sometimes become insecure at the thought of their mother being somewhere outside the world that they know about.'

'She might be, but if she is she's never said. And I've always worked, on and off, so why would it suddenly start being an issue for her now, when she was fine with it before? I'm always around when she comes home from school. I'm here whenever she needs me, although I might sometimes be asleep and need waking up. And if it was to do with my job why would she do these things to Amy and Tanya and Luke?'

'Maybe she's trying to get at you through them?' she suggested.

'Maybe.' I was growing weary of going round and round in the same circles.

She tried another idea. 'Could she be jealous of your friendship with Tanya?'

'Oh no, I'm sure she's not. She loves Tanya like a second mother,' I said. 'Sometimes I think she prefers her to me. Tanya is much better with little children than I am.'

All these things were possible, although I had never seen any sign of them before. Everything kept spinning round in my head, and none of it made any sense. I think I was hoping Sarah would just snap out of it. So many things that you worry about with children, like colic or bed-wetting or thumb-sucking, all just stop when the child is ready, so maybe she would just grow out of whatever it was that was troubling her mentally, just like David had grown out of his wild phase.

But the incidents grew worse and more frequent. Luke discovered all his favourite clothes slashed, and she even cut her own quilt covers. It was as if she thought she could put us off the scent if she destroyed some of her own things as well, suggesting that it must be someone else doing all the damage. It seemed like a transparent ploy because who else could it be? Unless it was Luke, and that seemed even less likely. He was behaving so sweetly about the whole thing. He would become momentarily angry with her when he discovered his things broken or torn, but he was still so protective of her whenever I got cross, as if he understood that she couldn't help what she was doing, that it was like some sort of illness. He wouldn't let anyone else be horrible to her.

'If anyone picks on you at school,' Luke would say to her, 'you tell me and I'll get them.'

Amy was almost as loyal, seemingly unable to believe that her friend was doing such terrible things. It almost made me feel worse that everyone was being so understanding and kind. When I heard them being so protective and loving, it made me want to cry, and I would

feel a flash of guilt that I wasn't being as unquestion-
ingly loyal to her as they were. Sometimes I would even
get cross with Luke when a new piece of damage was
discovered among his possessions.

'If you leave your stuff lying around, it's going to get
broken!' I would rant. 'You've got to take responsibility
for your own things.'

But I wasn't being fair to him because he wasn't leaving
his stuff around any more than the rest of us, or any
more than any other untidy little boy. In fact, he was
very good at looking after his things. And, even if he
should have been tidier, he still didn't deserve to suffer
these malicious attacks. I was flailing around, looking for
anyone to blame, trying to find any way I could to make
it harder for Sarah to do any more damage. She was so
clever at finding new ways to get round anything we did
to try to stop her. We had locked up every blade and
sharp implement we could find, but still she seemed to
be able to get hold of some new weapon.

I went to Primark one day to replace some of the
clothes that had been ruined. When I went to take them
out of the bag the next day, I found a kitchen fork lying
on top of them, and I knew before I even looked at the
clothes that Sarah must have used it to gouge the material. I hadn't even got round to taking the labels off and

already she had destroyed them. It was like trying to dam an unstoppable flood; the more we attempted to plug the holes, the more the water spilled over the top and round the sides. I tried to think of when she would have had time to get to the bag without anyone around and I could only think it must have been when I went to the bathroom (sometimes I do go in there with a book, just for a few minutes' peace and solitude). But I could hardly be expected to mount a guard on her every second of the time she was in the house. Or should I? Was I being a neglectful mother? Would someone who ran a more orderly household be able to keep a lid on this sort of thing?

Tanya and I now searched Sarah's room regularly when she was at school and we would find things like tweezers and toenail clippers hidden away for future use.

'How does a child of six think of these things?' I kept saying, over and over again. 'I would never think of using nail clippers to cut things up! Have I given birth to some sort of evil genius?'

Tanya would try to comfort me, but even she was finding it harder and harder to find encouraging things to say about the situation. There comes a time when cheerful optimism starts to sound like false bravado.

We gave Luke a padlock for his bedroom door, and

put another on ours, making sure that Sarah didn't find out the combinations. It was a horrible feeling to have to undo a padlock in order to get into your own bedroom.

Because, as you have doubtless gathered by now, I am rather a slapdash person, I don't always deal with my washing the moment it is ready. There are, I will readily admit, a few piles of clothes, both dirty and clean, sitting around the house. Some are waiting to go down to the wash, some are waiting to be loaded into the machine, some are waiting to be folded and ironed, some are waiting to be put away (which sometimes doesn't happen before they are used again and then come back into the never-ending cycle).

As a result, when I came across something that had been damaged, I often couldn't tell exactly how long it had been like that. Had it been done that day? Or several days before and only just come to light? In a busy family home, with people coming and going all the time, it was impossible to remember exactly how many minutes Sarah might have been on her own in any particular room on any particular day. We would need CCTV in every room if we were going to work out when and how she was going to strike next.

What was spookiest of all was that she was so cunning

in her campaign of destruction that no one ever actually caught her in the act. It showed that she was sly and clever and dangerous in a way that I had never imagined any child of mine could ever be. She had always been the most forthright and straightforward of little girls, sometimes too forthright for her own good! I couldn't recognise this silent, invisible vandal as the little baby I'd carried in my womb and given birth to. I had believed I had good instincts about people, that I could tell the good ones from the bad, and was disappointed to think that I must be so blinded by irrational maternal instincts that I had made such a fundamental misjudgement of Sarah's character. How many other people had I misjudged? Was the whole world laughing at me behind my back as I wandered around like Pollyanna, thinking the best of everyone?

Our once happy-go-lucky home took on a terrible atmosphere as the weeks turned into months, haunted by a mixture of hurt and anger, fear and distrust. There were always accusations and denials flying around. The air was heavy with suspicion and misery, and everywhere you turned, there were locks.

'Where have you been?' I would demand if Sarah had just been out of the room for five minutes.

'What have you been doing?'

'Where did you get that from?'

'Were you given that or did you take it?'

'What have you done now?'

It got so I could hardly bear the sound of my own voice. I didn't know what I would have done without Tanya's constant support and friendship. No matter how badly Sarah behaved towards us all, she continued to be on our side, ready to listen and sympathise, and to help in any way she could. She never criticised or suggested that it was our fault as bad parents, she just remained resolutely there for us. Who else would have been willing to listen to me going on and on for hours about my demon child?

Once I'd realised the school nurse had no more idea what could be going wrong than I did, I tried ringing social services. I knew they'd let Tanya down in the past, but now I was desperate and maybe this time I would come across someone who would be able to help. I felt I needed to explain to them that I was near the end of my tether and didn't know what I should be doing next – my daughter seemed to be turning into some sort of monster and I had no idea why. The strain was becoming almost intolerable, despite the pills the doctor was giving me for my nerves and my depression, and I was scared I might snap and lash out at Sarah in a moment of frustrated anger when I was confronted yet again by her apparent indifference to the damage she was doing to the family.

Each time I rang social services, I would find myself speaking to someone different and would have to explain the whole story again right from the start. And the more often I described Sarah's behaviour, the more ludicrous it sounded and the more difficult to understand. Each time they would come up with all the same suggestions as the nurse and everyone else, asking if there was any-thing that might be upsetting her, but I still couldn't think of anything. I suppose that I thought the more people I spoke to who had experience of some level of childcare, the more likely it was that I would stumble across some magical explanation, but in reality I only became more and more disillusioned with the sort of people who worked in these jobs. I was beginning to believe they didn't know any more than I did, and that is a horrible thought, like the first time it dawns on you that there is nothing your mother or father can do to heal the cut on your knee or your broken heart when your first boyfriend dumps you. If no one else can help you, then you're on your own, and who wants to be reminded of that during the bad times?

Each morning I would wake up with a renewed

determination to find the answer. If I could just work out *why* she was doing these things, maybe I would be able to see a way of stopping her.

One afternoon Tanya was round at my house and we were in the sitting room, talking as usual about the subject that had come to dominate my whole life.

'I'll make us a cup of tea,' Tanya said, and walked through to the kitchen. I was so grateful to her at moments like this, when she seemed to read my mind and know exactly what I needed. As I sat, staring out through the patio doors, past Mike's cluttered office space in the conservatory, to the grey skies beyond, there was a loud bang and all the lights went out. Even the hum of the fish tank fell silent as the illuminated water went black.

'Oh my God, Lyndsey,' Tanya screamed from the kitchen, 'I just switched on the kettle! What happened?'

I ran through to see if she was all right. She was obviously shaken, but didn't seem to have been hurt. I couldn't understand what had happened. We examined the kettle, but it looked fine.

'Tell me again what you did,' I said. 'Go through it step by step.'

'I just flicked on these two switches,' she said, 'because I wasn't sure which one was the kettle.'

I looked again at the socket she was pointing to. The kettle was plugged into one side and the Hoover into the other. I followed the lead along to where the Hoover was standing in the next room, and had been for some time as I hadn't been in much of a mood for cleaning, and saw there was a knife lying on the floor, the blade still in the flex, having cut half the way through it. I pulled the plug out of the wall and lifted the knife. Examining the blade, I could see that the electric current had actually burnt a hole through the metal in the split second before fusing the whole house.

'How did she get this?' I asked, my hand shaking. 'Every knife in the house is locked up! I can't believe it! How is she doing this?'

'My God, I could have been killed,' Tanya wailed, her hands trembling.

I sorted out the fuses and made Tanya a cup of tea, settling her down on the sofa. I didn't know what to say. She was right — she could have been killed. My worst nightmares were becoming real: if Sarah could do this in her own home, what might she do at school or in other people's houses? How would we ever recover if she actually killed someone, or maimed them for life, or burnt their house down?

This was so frightening I was past feeling angry. When

Sarah got home I sat her down and quietly asked her if it had been her. This was too serious for histrionics; I had to keep it sensible. She swore that it wasn't.

'Do you realise how dangerous it is to mess around with electricity?' I asked.

'Yes, Mummy,' she said indignantly. 'I've learned about it at school. You must always turn the electricity off before you touch anything electric, otherwise you get a shock and that could kill you.'

She was looking me directly in the eyes as she talked and I couldn't see the slightest flicker of guilt. At that moment, I believed her. I couldn't imagine that she was lying to me, she seemed so honest and genuine. But how else could it have happened? Was she such a good liar that she could do it without the slightest blush or tremor? What hope did we have if she was that skilful?

That evening, after Sarah had gone to bed, I sat down with Mike and tried to work out possible ways the knife could have come to be embedded in the wire. As the wire was useless now anyway, I tried to cut through it myself with the same knife, but I wasn't able to do it with the same neat line that the initial cut had made. So how could Sarah, with her little hands, have sawn such a straight line? I tried to work out if there was any way that the knife could have fallen off the work surface on to the wire and cut halfway through it on landing. Even as I was thinking about it, I knew it was a ridiculous idea, but what other explanation could there be?

'No.' Mike shook his head with a bit of a wry smile at my ignorance. 'That wouldn't be possible.' But with all his practical knowledge, he still couldn't come up with any alternative explanation. It had to have been done on purpose, and Sarah was the only suspect in the frame.

Nevertheless, I sat there for ages trying to work out some possible logical explanation for what had happened. It was just so hard to believe that either of my children could have done such a stupid and dangerous thing, but I couldn't find any explanation at all, just as I hadn't been able to fathom Sarah's other behaviour. It was so frustrating and so humbling. We all like to think there is an answer to every problem, but supposing there just weren't any answers to this one? Nothing seemed to make sense any more and I felt a shiver of apprehension at the thought of what might go wrong next.

13

My Bad Parenting

As I'm too lazy to carry the Hoover up and down the stairs every time I need it, I keep another one upstairs to do the bedrooms. A few days later I found that the wire for this one had been cut in exactly the same way as the downstairs one. Yet again I was amazed that Sarah had been able to execute such a clean cut, but still I couldn't come up with any alternative explanation for how it could have happened, unless we were being haunted by some sort of poltergeist.

Tanya was incredibly supportive all through this latest development in our family trauma, even though she felt her own life had been threatened by the first instance of wire cutting. I realised how lucky I was that it hadn't happened to anyone else, who might have sued me if they had actually received a shock. I also knew that Tanya wouldn't go round the area gossiping about things that happened within the privacy of our own homes. It had taken her long enough to get round to sharing some of her own secrets with me, let alone anyone else's.

Tanya knew how isolated and desperate I was starting to feel and she made sure to ring me at least once a day, often more, just as she had for so long.

'Have you found anything else yet?' would be her first question on almost every call. I almost wished she would talk about something else, to distract me from the fears and bewilderment that were befuddling my brain, making it hard to get on with enjoying any of the other parts of my life. But I was grateful for her concern anyway, and for all the hours she was willing to put in helping me to search Sarah's things, and watch her when she wasn't in school.

'I'm not looking any more,' I told her at one stage, when she asked the inevitable question. 'I just don't want to deal with any new revelations at the moment.'

It was all becoming too emotionally charged, more than I could handle without endangering my own mental health, and I wanted to distance myself from it, pretend it wasn't happening, at least for a few hours a day. Maybe I was being a bit of an ostrich and sticking my head in the sand in the vain hope that if I didn't find anything the whole situation would disappear, but sometimes you have to do that in order not to go completely mad. We all need to escape from reality every now and again; if we didn't, we wouldn't need to drink, or watch television and the movies, or even read books. Reality can be a bit gruelling twenty-four hours a day.

Then I began to think that maybe I was blocking out a lot more things than I realised. Sometimes Tanya would be with me as I was sorting through my washing and she would spot little nicks and cuts that I hadn't seen. I do tend to be very slapdash about these sorts of chores and she is much more meticulous, but on top of that I think I was deliberately not focusing on things, not wanting to see them for what they really were. I was so desperate for life to go back to normal to the extent that I wouldn't see what was in front of me. But it was becoming increasingly difficult to ignore.

'It's no good you denying that it's you doing all these things,' I said to Sarah one evening after yet another incident. 'We keep finding stuff in your room, so it must be you.'

She just looked at me without saying anything. It

didn't even look as if her eyes were watering up, which they normally did when we had these talks. Usually, whenever we discussed what she was doing, she wouldn't be able to stop her eyes filling with tears that would soon start pouring unstoppably down her cheeks. It would break my heart to see it. Sometimes she even cried without making a noise, or talked to me quite normally while she was doing it. It made me all the more desperate to get to the bottom of whatever it was that was troubling her so much. To see my baby weeping helplessly like that was almost too much to bear.

But it was worse in a way to see her dry-eyed. It was as though her heart was toughening up and she was running out of tears to cry.

'It is you, isn't it?' I pressed.

'Yes.' She nodded solemnly, with no flicker of emotion in her eyes.

'Why are you doing it?' I asked, knowing what the answer would be.

'I don't know.'

'Are you unhappy about anything?'

She shook her head.

'So why do you want to keep tearing things and taking things and breaking things?'

'I don't know!' she shouted, and stormed out of the

room in exasperation at my insistence. We were both desperately tired of me asking the same questions over and over again.

I was growing more and more certain that she was telling the truth. She really didn't know why she was doing it, and that was a horrible thought. It was as though we were all living with a dangerous stranger, even Sarah.

───────────

Mike always spends a lot of time on his computer, both for work and entertainment, so he was worried when his new cordless mouse disappeared. He knew he wouldn't have mislaid it.

'Have you taken Daddy's mouse?' I asked Sarah.

She nodded, with the same faraway look in her eyes that I'd seen when I last asked her why she was doing these things.

'Where have you put it?' I asked, expecting her to say she didn't know, as usual.

'I think I chucked it in the bushes.' She pointed to the garden, speaking completely matter-of-factly, as if there was nothing odd about taking someone else's possession, throwing it away and then owning up to it.

Mike sighed and went out to search for it.

'Which bush, Sarah?' he asked.

'That one, I think.' She was squinting at the garden as if trying to recall a memory that was eluding her.

Mike searched the shrub she was pointing to, but there was no mouse.

'Maybe it was that one,' she suggested, pointing rather doubtfully to another one. With admirable patience and restraint, Mike searched everywhere she directed him. I think, like me, he could sense that she was doing her best to be helpful, and was as disappointed as he was when each suggestion proved to be wrong. Our garden is not large and it didn't take long to exhaust all the possibilities. Neither of us could work out if she was deliberately teasing us or if she genuinely couldn't remember what she had done with it. There were always so many elements of doubt in every situation we came up against.

While Mike was as concerned as I was about the transformation of our daughter, he wasn't comfortable talking about it, and tried to shut it out as much as he could. I'm sure he was grateful to Tanya for being willing to listen to me for hours on end. Men, I've noticed, are never keen to talk about things that don't have a solution. Come up with a problem they can solve there and then and they are perfectly happy; present them with something which is a little bit more open-ended and they begin to find it frustrating. Their attention starts to wander, and, in my experience, long sessions of listening is not a male strong point. When Sarah's behaviour started to affect Mike's work, however, he could no longer pretend it wasn't happening. He might have been able to ignore shredded curtains and clothes, but a lost mouse was something altogether closer to his heart.

In my continuing quest for someone with some answers, I took Sarah to see the educational psychologist at school.

'I expect you're one of these parents who give in to their children's every whim,' he said, after listening to my concerns for a bit, 'so they don't have to earn the right to anything.'

'Am I?' I asked, surprised to be judged so quickly and damningly. I couldn't claim he was completely wrong, but I didn't think I was that bad.

'If you carry on like this, by the time she's sixteen you'll be getting a phone call to tell you she's pregnant or on drugs,' he went on, sounding more like some evangelist preacher of hellfire and damnation than a professional psychologist.

I might have actually reeled back when he made these terrible predictions – I certainly felt like I did. I suppressed my instinctive desire to answer back and defend my child-rearing record: after all, I wanted to point out, we had treated Luke just the same and he wasn't exhibiting any of these abnormalities. I told myself I had gone there to hear some expert advice, so it was no good complaining if I didn't like what I heard. I must be willing to accept that I might be the one at fault here, be a grown-up and take it on the chin. I took several deep breaths and held my temper in check.

I went away that day determined to take on board his advice and to try to be a more responsible and thoughtful parent. His comment wasn't completely without justification. I knew that sometimes I was inconsistent, giving in to the children's nagging after initially saying 'no' to something. I'd always put it down to my own ability to see when I might be wrong in my first answers and my willingness to change. I had always told myself that it was a character strength to be flexible rather than a weakness. I had watched other parents who would take a stand on something and then refuse to budge, even when it was obvious they were wrong, forcing their children to rebel over stupid little things, and I had hoped my approach was more intelligent than that. Was I fooling myself? Was I just being weak and lazy, as he suggested? Perhaps my flexibility was really just a desire for a quiet life.

All right then, I resolved, I'll put an end to all that. From now on, I'm going to be stricter, wiser and more consistent. If my parenting skills are so bad that they've sent Sarah completely off the rails, then I'll do what I can to improve.

It was hard to accept that I really had been such a bad mother, but I was willing to do anything to be better and help Sarah get well. If I firmed up on the family guidelines and generally got more of a grip on things, maybe I could still lick this thing before somebody got killed or our family disintegrated.

These flashes of optimism never lasted long.

Despite my new-found resolve, Sarah's activities continued. Two Sky cards went missing from the television. Then my car keys and the house keys disappeared, which meant we had to spend hours getting them all replaced, not knowing if they would turn up the moment we'd gone to all the expense and trouble. Luke's GameBoy was damaged and found in Sarah's room, just as his phone had been when she broke that. The family paddling pool was slashed. More and more I puzzled over how Sarah was so clever that she never got caught, and was never seen doing a single one of her damaging acts of vandalism. What was more, I couldn't understand how such a clever operator was then careless enough to leave the evidence in her room for us to find so easily.

Sooner or later, I thought, we would catch her in the act and we would be able to confront her with the evidence of what she was doing, making it impossible for her to keep blocking our questions with 'Don't know'. As long as she was managing to do everything in secret, we didn't know whether she was in some kind of trance when she did these things, like a sleepwalker or someone hypnotised, or whether she was pulling the wool over our eyes and knew exactly what she was doing.

We were all becoming accustomed to living in a kind of *Alice in Wonderland* world where nothing made sense – it's amazing how quickly you adapt to the strangest circumstances. Things were no longer what they seemed, and the normal rules of logic didn't apply any more.

When the remote control for the television went missing, we started on another laborious search of the whole house, from top to bottom. If things like this didn't turn up immediately in Sarah's room, experience told us they would not turn up at all. But we tried anyway. As he likes to watch television in comfort, and is not keen on having to jump up and down every time he wants to change channels, Mike joined in this search. When we had looked in every possible nook and cranny we could think of, with Sarah making bright suggestions every now and then of somewhere else she thought she might have put it, Mike went into the bathroom. For some reason, he decided to lift the lid on the toilet cistern and there it was, lying in the water. Maybe he remembered the scene in *The Godfather* where Al Pacino fishes the gun out of the cistern in order to execute a couple of enemies; so many of the scenes we were playing out in our house were like something from the movies.

Sarah was in my bedroom with me when he brought it in, drying it on a towel.

'Oh look, Sarah,' he said, with heavy sarcasm, 'I've found the remote control.'

Sarah looked up from whatever she was doing and said, 'Mum, where's my skirt?'

She completely blanked him out, as if she hadn't heard a word. It seemed she could no longer even bring herself to talk about her problem. She'd told us, over and over and over again, that she didn't know why she was breaking and stealing things and that she was never able to remember doing it, and now she could no longer be bothered to even protest her innocence. I could only guess that it was a self-protection mechanism. If she couldn't do anything to stop herself from doing these things, then she would just pretend they weren't happening. To us, when what we wanted more than anything was to be able to communicate with her and find out what was going on, this was just another layer of frustration. Her lack of interest made it look as if she was being arrogant and didn't care about the damage she was doing to the family and her friends. But the more we tried to get through to her, the more she blanked us, and the more we sounded like nagging bores.

Bearing in mind what the educational psychologist had told me, I decided I must have a firm strategy regarding punishments for the crimes she was committing. I decided the consequences must always be short and sharp and must not be allowed to linger on. So I might take Luke swimming and make Sarah stay at home if one of her misdemeanours had just been uncovered, or I might ban her from going on a school trip. Once the punishment was over, however, that would be the end of it and we would try to get back to normal. I would then do something nice with her in an attempt to reward the good behaviour and not just punish the bad. The pattern would always be the same: a crime would be uncovered; I would ask her if she was guilty and she would either admit it, shrug or completely ignore the question, which I would take as an admission of guilt; I would then tell her what her punishment would be.

'OK,' she would say, without a flicker of emotion, as if she had accepted that it was pointless to protest her innocence any longer and that it would be easier for her to just accept the inevitable and get it over and done with as quickly as possible.

What broke my heart was that I could see that nothing I was doing was making any difference. If there was something making her unhappy, driving her to act this way, then I was probably making her even more unhappy with the punishments. But what was the alternative? Textbook answers are all very well, until they don't work, because then you have nowhere left to go.

Sometimes there would be a couple of weeks when nothing would happen and I would begin to hope that it had all just been a maturational hiccup and that we were through to the other side.

'Everything seems to be going better now,' I would tell Tanya when she asked. 'We seem to be getting on much better again, thank God.'

But it never lasted.

14

Secrets and Lies

As well as going round one another's houses, and talking on the phone, Tanya and I also used to meet in chat rooms on the Internet. I'd become rather addicted to chat rooms; I suppose it was another way of escaping the nightmare at home for a few hours, entering a semi-imaginary other world where I could tell people as much or as little about myself as I wanted. I was well aware that I didn't always know who I was talking to, and that people might sometimes not be exactly who they said they were, but on the whole I am a very trusting person and so I tended to assume they were telling the truth about themselves until I discovered otherwise.

Being so trusting meant that I would sometimes get really cross with Tanya when I discovered that she was talking to me while pretending to be someone else as a joke. I hated those sorts of games and told her so, but sometimes she just didn't seem to be able to resist winding me up. It was a testament to how strong our friendship was that she could do something deliberately to annoy me, and it wouldn't affect our basic relationship. I always felt able to tell her openly when I was cross with her, so bad feelings were never able to take root or fester.

In the course of our many long conversations, both on and off the screen, she started to open up more about her past and about the abuse she had suffered as a child, which she had hinted at early on in our relationship, but which she had never said any more about at the time. Around the time when David was out of control, when it seemed that other parts of her life returned to haunt her, Tanya had told me the awful stories about the abuse inside her family, but since then she hadn't talked about it. I have to admit I had been a bit cowardly and had deliberately avoided the area for as long as possible, knowing that releasing those sorts of memories can be very traumatic for people, and feeling that Tanya and I had enough to contend with without opening another can of worms unnecessarily.

As my own problems with Sarah were increasing, Tanya began dropping hints that she had further dark secrets to reveal to me. I think one of the reasons she liked to communicate through Internet chat rooms was because she found it easier to talk about really painful subjects when we weren't actually in a room together. It's sometimes easier to write something down than it is to speak it out loud. I could tell there was a lot that she still hadn't told me.

'You'll hate me if you find out the sort of person I really am,' was one of her favourite sayings, and it felt as though she was begging me to deny it.

'I won't hate you,' I would assure her obligingly. 'I know what you're like, you've been my best friend for years. I don't care what you've done in the past, and I know you wouldn't do anything that would affect me or my family.'

But I still didn't press her to go into any more detail and it took her ages to find the courage to start talking. Once she did start, however, she soon developed a pattern of behaviour, which meant I would always know when there was something she needed to get off her chest. If we were at my house or her house together, she would begin hyperventilating dramatically, as if she was having some sort of panic attack, and I would know that she was going to tell me something from her past.

Then Tanya would start talking, but in a quite different voice to her normal one. This was the high, piping voice of a child, and I found it very frightening, as if she was possessed by some dead child's spirit, acting as its mouthpiece on earth. She would begin to tell me experiences of her childhood as though she had actually regressed and gone back there.

During one of these conversations, she was having so much trouble breathing that I rang our local surgery and asked if it would be all right to give her some of the Propranolol tablets the doctor had prescribed to me for my own panic attacks. They said it would be fine, and the medication did seem to calm Tanya down. When she eventually found the strength to explain to me what had happened in a way that I could understand, she told me a terrible story that made my heart ache with pity for her. A man had started abusing her when she was only four years old.

'He used to play this game with a coin,' she said, 'and somehow the coin would always end up in my knickers. He was very good at making me think that it was me who wanted to play these games, not him. I loved him and I wanted to please him and I knew that it made him feel good when I let him do these things.'

'Oh, Tanya,' I said, filled with horror and finding it difficult to know what to say. 'That's terrible – you poor little thing. It wasn't your fault, you do know that, don't you?'

From what I had heard about child abuse, this man's games sounded like the sort of technique a paedophile might use to win a child's cooperation. Difficult as it was to listen to the vile acts that Tanya had suffered as a child, it seemed to help her to talk about it.

She told me that this was before the abuse by her father began; in fact, one form of abuse had led to another. First this man had played his nasty games with her, and then he passed her on to a number of paedophiles in the area where they lived. They had taken it in turns to abuse her all through her childhood. I had heard how that happened to some children, how they seemed to acquire the stamp of 'victim' on them in some way and found themselves constantly falling into the same trap. These poor mites began to think that this was the normal thing to happen, that it was simply the way life was, and began to accept it.

'I was eight when I got the courage to tell my dad about what was happening to me,' she whispered. 'I told him about the abusers, so he asked me to show him what they did to me. That's when he started too.'

'Oh, Tanya.' I held her hand. I still found it so hard to believe that her father, whom I'd met so often and seemed such a nice old man who couldn't do enough to help Tanya when she needed it, was the sort of person who would sexually abuse his own daughter, but I knew that it was sometimes just the kind of people you most trusted that were something quite different underneath.

'I told my mum, and she believed me at first. But when I told her that it was Dad as well, she wouldn't believe me, and called me a liar.'

I felt very sorry for Tanya and wanted to do something to help her cope with the trauma of the memories. I didn't know how to advise her myself, so I went to the library to find books on dealing with childhood abuse. She made me promise not to tell anyone else her secrets and, even though the stories she was telling me were so dreadful I could hardly bear to hear them, I was proud that she trusted me, and me alone, with such personal stuff. What alarmed me was that I wasn't equipped to help her with the dreadful burden of what had happened to her in the past. But I would never tell anyone, if that was what she wanted, and she knew me well enough to be able to trust me. I would never divulge her secrets.

The more she talked, the more complicated I realised

her life was. There were whole sections of Tanya's existence that she had kept hidden from me for all these
years and was gradually now revealing. It made sense
that she had learned to keep these painful things secret,
as abuse victims often can. It also made sense that the
cycle of abuse continued, as it so often does, with one
thing leading to the next.

She told me about a man called Frank, who was
stalking her. He was a childhood friend who'd become
her boyfriend for a while before she met Andrew. Now
he was a menacing man, dangerous and often violent,
and he knew where she lived. When Andrew was out,
he would turn up at the house and sometimes he would
hit her. Andrew had started doing some decorating work
for Mike and was often out of the house at the time when
she first began to tell me about Frank.

'He hates me because of what I did to him,' she told
me, through heartbroken sobs.

'What did you do?' I asked, unable to imagine what
she could have done to make a man so angry with her
for so long.

'When I was being abused as a child, the men who were
abusing me asked me to bring a friend to meet them. I
was terrified and didn't know what to do. They forced
me; they told me that awful things would happen to me

if I didn't obey. Of course I didn't want to do it – but in the end, I brought Frank along, even though he didn't want to go. I don't think he has ever forgiven me. I know it was bad but I was only a child and I didn't know what else to do. I feel so guilty about it, but honestly, Lyndsey, I had no choice. But he doesn't understand that, even though I've told him a million times how sorry I am. He still wants to punish me. He'll never leave me alone.'

I was stunned by this new turn of events. Previously, Tanya's awful troubles seemed confined to her past, long before her marriage and the arrival of her children. Now, her past had stepped terrifyingly into the present. In all the years I had been listening to other people's troubles, I had never heard of something so terrible and so frightening.

'How does Frank know when Andrew's out, so it's safe for him to come round to the house?' I asked, after a few moments. 'Do you tell him?'

'I don't know how he knows,' she said. 'He just turns up. He must be watching the house.'

To my shame, I was frightened then for myself and my family as well. Would this mysterious and violent Frank turn up while I was at her house? I'm not a brave person and a bit of a coward when it comes to my own personal safety. I told myself not to be so wet. What have *you* got to worry about? I rebuked myself. It's Tanya who's really suffering. Look how brave and strong she is, after all this has happened. Get a grip.

One day when I was at home on my own the phone rang. It was Tanya.

'It's taken me ages to dial you,' she gasped. 'You've got to help me. Can you come and untie me?'

'What do you mean?' I thought I must have misheard her.

'Frank has just been down and he's left me tied up,' she sobbed.

'Is he there?' I asked nervously.

'No, it's all right, he's gone.'

With my heart in my mouth, I hurried round, convinced this man was going to spring out at me at any moment. What had he done to Tanya? Had he hurt her? I knew I had to overcome my fear and help her as soon as I could if there was any chance at all that she was in danger.

I let myself into the house, calling Tanya's name as I went.

'Lyndsey! Help me! I'm up here.' A pitiful voice came down from upstairs.

I hurried up the stairs, my heart thumping and adrenalin coursing through me. I was frightened of what I would find but I had no choice: I had to go to Tanya.

The bathroom door was ajar and I pushed it open with a shaking hand. The scene that confronted me was like something from a movie. Tanya was lying on the floor, curled up, the phone lying near her face. She was staring up at me with a wild expression of panic and helplessness, and her wrists and ankles were bound with rope.

'Oh my God,' I gasped. 'Are you all right?'

'I'm fine, he didn't hurt me too badly,' she said. 'Can you help me?'

I hurried to her and started trying to undo the knots. She told me that Frank had flown into a rage and tied her up as a punishment.

Once I established that she was not hurt, I started to feel less frightened and instead I became furious on her behalf.

'For God's sake, Tanya,' I said, as I struggled with the rope, 'this is serious! I mean it. This is assault, it's not something you can excuse no matter how you look at it. How long are you going to be a victim for? You have got to put a stop to this man's activities.'

I was angry to see her like this, the victim of a violent man who could treat her in this appalling way. I couldn't bear that Tanya should suffer like this.

She whimpered and didn't reply. At once, I felt guilty

for laying straight into her when she had just been through such an obviously traumatic ordeal. She needed sympathy, not an interrogation.

'How did you manage to ring me?' I asked, trying to piece together in my mind what must have happened.

'I used my nose to dial,' she explained. 'But it took ages to get it right.'

Although I had made a point of trying not to offer advice, merely lending a sympathetic ear, I began to feel strongly that she had to do something about this man, or else the abuse would keep going on and on. If she never made a stand, when would he stop? Could he take it further and hurt her seriously? There was no excuse for continuing to punish Tanya for a childhood grudge, however deeply rooted it might be.

'You've got to go to the police,' I told her firmly. 'They can stop it. They can make him go away. This is a serious matter, Tanya. I'll back you up.'

'No, no,' she protested, almost frantic. 'I can't go to the police. Don't make me go. I'm frightened of what Frank will do if he finds out.'

'They can help you, Tanya!'

'No! No!' She began to sound hysterical and tears sprang into her eyes.

I wanted to cry too, seeing my friend reduced to this,

fearful and victimised in her own home. But I couldn't go against her wishes and decided to back down.

'All right, all right, it's OK.' I tried to calm her, hiding my own feelings of distress. 'You're fine. We won't tell anyone, don't worry.'

Once she was free of her binds, I helped her downstairs and made her a cup of tea to help her get over the shock, and tried to work out what I should do. I no longer felt very confident of my own opinion. The things going on at home with Sarah were enough to undermine my old confidence that I had some kind of notion of how to work out problems. Even less was I able to deal with someone who was clearly traumatised by the dreadful events that had happened to her in the past. If Tanya didn't want the police to find out, then that was her decision. I could only stand by her, as she always stood by me in the hard times, and help her as best I could.

But it was hard to listen to what was happening to her, and feel so powerless. Frank was still coming round to the house, and Tanya kept on letting him in. Despite the awful things he was doing to her every time he went round, she refused to go to the police and appeared terrified when I suggested it.

Sometimes I felt angry with Tanya for allowing him to do these things to her. But I understood that sometimes childhood abuse can cause enormous damage to the victims in later life, and so I didn't push her too hard and I continued to listen as she gradually revealed more and more of the terrible events of her past. It was shocking to think that someone who was as strong as she was in so many ways could be undermined so easily by something that had been done to her years earlier. It was hard to imagine how someone who could so completely dominate her husband, could allow another man to hold so much power over her. Just like the problems with Sarah, I simply couldn't get my brain round it. Nothing seemed to be making sense to me any more. I was back with Alice in Wonderland, just lurching from one surreal experience to the next.

15

Inside Sarah's Mind

I thought it was very important all along that I kept the school informed of what was happening inside the family. I wanted to be as honest as possible with them, so that they would be able to keep an eye on Sarah when she was with them, for her own protection and other people's. I wanted to know if she was being bullied, but I also wanted them to make sure she didn't get a chance to endanger anyone else's children. After a good bit of soul-searching, I told them about the wire-cutting incident, explaining that I couldn't see how it could have been her, but that I hadn't been able to find any other explanation. The school nurse could obviously see that

I was now deeply worried and referred me to the Child and Adolescent Mental Health Team.

This sounded to me like we were moving a whole rung up the ladder. What would happen if they told me Sarah was going insane? Would it be a relief to know that there was actually something medically wrong, or would it just be worse to realise that my child had mental problems? And would that mean they would take her away from me, section her and put her into an institution? I couldn't decide which was going to be the worst option: to be told Sarah was mad or to be told they had no idea what was wrong.

When I rang up to find out when they could see us, they told me that Sarah had gone straight up to number three on the waiting list, which was quite unusual. It seemed the authorities were starting to take this seriously, which was comforting in one way, reassuring me that I wasn't imagining the extent of all of this, but in another way, more deeply frightening, as the cogs of officialdom started turning.

While we were waiting for the appointment to come round, I tried really hard to stay off Sarah's case. I wanted her to think that I trusted her and was on her side. But my worries kept getting the better of me and I found it hard to be with her without nagging or checking up on what she was doing. Tanya was really good at coming round and taking the pressure off me by spending time with Sarah, playing with her, talking to her or just doing something simple and soothing like combing her hair. Sarah appreciated the attention and often told Tanya how much she loved her. I should have been able to do more of that sort of thing myself, but I was always so agitated and on edge, it was hard for me to be a calming influence on anyone.

'God, you're a much better mum than I am,' I would tell Tanya after she'd spent hours patiently listening to Sarah prattling on about some nonsense. 'I'm finding it hard to even be nice to her any more after all the lying and spiteful things she's done to everyone.'

'She's still the same Sarah,' Tanya reminded me. 'We still love her, don't we?'

'Of course,' I snapped defensively. I wasn't going to stop loving my child just because there might be something wrong with her. I felt guilty for even giving Tanya that impression, and vowed to work harder to let Sarah know how much I loved her.

Sometimes it was easy. I would creep into her room late at night while she was sleeping and I would look down at her as she lay in bed, her hair spread out on the pillow, looking like the same kind, sweet, innocent little girl I had always believed her to be and I would feel an ache in my chest, as if my heart was actually bleeding for her and for whatever it was she was having to put up with in her head that was changing her personality so radically. I would watch her for a while in the vain hope that she would stand up and start walking about in her sleep, so I could see how she did all these awful things that it genuinely seemed she could not remember, but she never moved. As I stood there in the darkness, I wondered if the demon in her was able to sense that I was watching, and knew to wait until I had gone before rising. Once or twice I was unable to resist the temptation to lie down beside her and cuddle her until she woke up. She smelled so fresh and clean and lovely.

'I really love you, Sarah,' I whispered as she stirred.

'I love you too, Mummy,' she would reply sleepily, snuggling in, grateful for any moment of kindness at a time when everyone, including her own mother, seemed to spend most of the day shouting at her and being angry.

'Why are you so unhappy?' I murmured, hoping to catch her unawares while she was so sleepy and her guard was down. 'Tell Mummy and perhaps we can sort it out.'

'I don't know, Mummy. I don't know why I'm doing it.'

I knew I was driving her mad with my questions but I just couldn't stop myself from asking.

Our appointment with the mental health team came round and we did some sessions with just the therapist, Sarah and me. I found it difficult to talk about things in front of Sarah, and felt uncomfortable discussing her behaviour and what possible reasons there might be for it while she was sitting there listening. Not surprisingly, she didn't like being talked about either, and tended to get quite cross and gobby. I didn't really mind; although I didn't like it when she was rude in front of other people, at least it was normal behaviour for a child of her age.

The therapist was quite good at getting me to accept responsibility for my feelings and deal with them myself, rather than trying to rely on her to sort me out. It would have been so nice just to hand everything over to someone else and let them find the answers, but I knew that wasn't going to be possible. This was our problem and no one else's, we were going to have to find the cure.

'You know, Lyndsey,' the therapist said, after a few sessions, 'I come across a lot of very disturbed children, and Sarah isn't one of them. She's confident, a bit bossy perhaps, which isn't such a bad thing. She's obviously angry with you, but she seems quite happy to leave your side. She interacts well and isn't aggressive or angry in her general demeanour. In my opinion, she's a perfectly normal child.'

'Then why is she doing these things?' I asked, only half relieved by her conclusion.

'I don't know.'

That phrase again!

It was a comfort, though, that this woman, whose opinion I rated, agreed with my original assessment of Sarah. But if she was normal, what was making her do so many terrible things? I just wanted someone to be able to explain what was going on, but it didn't seem that anyone was going to be able to. I didn't know who to turn to next.

Maybe, I thought, just talking to the therapist will have had some effect on Sarah. Maybe she simply wanted to have her problems acknowledged. Maybe it would all now be over and we could go back to being a normal family.

I should have known better than to have allowed myself the luxury of such a dream after so many disappointments. Whenever I dared to think like that, things nearly always took a turn for the worse, and this time was no exception.

16

The Birthday Party

It was Sarah's seventh birthday and I organised a party for her. I wanted to make a real effort, to compensate her a little for all the horrible times she'd had to go through in the previous months. It's so easy to get into the habit of always being cross with a naughty child, which just makes you and the child feel worse. I was determined that Sarah should see how much we loved her and how nice life could be all the time if she could just stop doing the dreadful things that made everyone so unhappy.

I suspect I was also feeling a little bit guilty that as a mother I wasn't able to help my child, and I wanted to make it up to her. It was similar to when she was a baby and wouldn't stop crying. I would change her, feed her, give her a drink; I tried cuddling her, distracting her, doing everything I could to make her comfortable. When the screams kept going, I would eventually call the doctor and check there was nothing medically wrong. At that stage, I would start to feel desperate, my temper would fray and I would reach a dangerous point where I might lose it. If I had done everything I possibly could and the problem still persisted, I could start to feel, usually quite unreasonably, that it was the child's fault. With little babies, it is fairly easy to keep telling yourself that you must stay patient; with a child who should be able to tell you what the problem is, it's harder.

As her birthday treat, I invited five of her friends to come swimming, including Amy, even though I was nervous that Sarah might do something during the party that would result in them getting hurt.

I have to let her mix with other children, I told myself. What is the alternative? I can't keep her in isolation for the rest of her life! As long as I watch her like a hawk, everything will be fine.

At the swimming pool there was the added back-up of lifeguards, who would keep a vigilant eye on all the children. It was unlikely that Sarah would do anything there. Tanya very kindly offered to come and help me.

Everything went smoothly, with no unfortunate accidents in the water, and afterwards I took them down to an arcade to play on the games and amusements before having a McDonald's and returning to the house for a sleepover. I was beginning to feel optimistic that everything would work out fine, but I still didn't take my eyes off Sarah for a moment. It was great to see her having fun, laughing and shouting and talking nonsense as if she didn't have a care in the world, but every time she went near one of the others, I was straining to see if she was doing something sneaky or surreptitious. If she knew that I was right beside her at every turn, I thought, perhaps she would behave herself – but I couldn't be sure. I couldn't drop my guard for a second.

Tanya offered to stay the night with me to help with the clearing up once the girls had gone upstairs to bed. I was very grateful for the offer as it was hard to keep an eye on Sarah and do everything else that needed doing as well. Mike had decided to go overnight fishing with a friend to get out of the way; I don't think a house full of screaming seven-year-olds was a very attractive prospect and he jumped at the chance to get a bit of time and space to himself. I could understand why he felt he wanted a break from the constant stress and tension in the air at home. He must have been so fed up with listening to me going over and over my worries, and hearing what new vandalism Sarah had been up to. It was difficult for both of us and I can't pretend it didn't put our relationship under a strain. It seemed much easier for him to turn his back on the things that he didn't want to face than it was for me, and I felt that the entire responsibility for our family's welfare was on my shoulders. I would try to talk to him about it but he struggled when it came to discussing feelings. To be fair to him, I talked about very little else except our current problems and what suggestions he had were soon exhausted.

Despite everything, I appreciated the support he did give me in his own way, and I knew he would always be there for us. I didn't begrudge him a little time away from the atmosphere at home.

Mike loved his fishing and kept all his gear in a zipped bag. When he got to the river and settled down with the bag that evening, he discovered it had been cut in the same way as everything else in the house. So had his collapsible chair. His umbrella was cut as well, but we didn't discover that until a bit later, when I was sitting under it in the garden, reading in the rain and it started leaking on my book. Up until that point, Mike had been relatively untouched by Sarah's crusade. Very little of his stuff had been damaged, which suggested that Sarah wasn't as angry with him as she was with the rest of us. This development suggested that she was angry with all of us. In one way, I was relieved whenever Mike was forced to take notice of what was happening. I was always worried that he might think I was exaggerating or imagining things. Sometimes I was afraid that he might be right.

Back at the house, however, the party had gone well. I'd bought Sarah a little crop-top and a knicker set, both of which she seemed really pleased with. It was lovely to see her so happy. By the time we finally got all the children settled down and quiet enough so we could go to bed, Tanya and I were exhausted. I felt so relieved that we had managed to get through the whole evening without any disasters; no tears and no rows, just a happy, noisy time. I prayed she wouldn't get up to anything in the night while we were all asleep. It would be more difficult for her with so many people in the room, I thought. How would she step over them all without waking them up? Eventually I managed to relax and fall asleep.

The next morning, when the other kids had left and

she went to get dressed, Tanya discovered that her jeans had been cut while she was sleeping. I couldn't believe it. How had Sarah managed to do that without waking any of us? What had she used to do it? Further investigations revealed that Tanya's puffa jacket, which she had left draped over the banister, had also been slashed. Sarah must have been wandering all over the house in her sleep and we hadn't heard a thing. It was the same sort of small, straight cuts that had appeared in everything else so there was no doubt it was the same perpetrator. I felt so bad because I knew Tanya was fond of that outfit, as she hardly ever wore anything else, even in the middle of summer. It had been so kind of her to offer to help and this was how we repaid her.

There was the usual confrontation and the usual blank reaction from Sarah. It hardly seemed worth even getting cross with her any more. It never did any good. I almost felt like I was becoming as resigned to this sort of thing as she was.

When I went into Sarah's room to look for something a few days later, I found her new crop-top on the floor with a great big hole torn in it. The weight of the world seemed to land on my shoulders and a bleak depression settled over me. I took it back downstairs to show Tanya, who was having a cup of coffee. I could still picture the little birthday girl of a few days before, who had been so happy when she opened the parcel and saw that it was exactly what she had wanted. She had been so excited and so grateful and now the gift had been destroyed by this other part of her. I couldn't stop crying.

After all these months, things were just getting worse and we were no nearer to finding out the cause of the problem. I have to admit, I felt almost as sorry for myself as I did for Sarah. I had been so pleased with the way she had behaved at the party. Why would she deliberately spoil a present I had gone to so much trouble to buy for her? Why would any sane person do that?

The sight of that ripped crop-top was too much for my self-control and I lost my temper. I was back to screaming and shouting at Sarah, and she was screaming and shouting back. She seemed as upset by the damage as she was by my accusations.

'I didn't do it! I didn't do it!' she yelled.

'But it's in your room,' I shouted back, 'like everything else! Who else would have done it?'

'I don't know! I don't know!'

Tanya sat quietly watching, waiting for us both to run out of steam. Although I was embarrassed for anyone to see and hear us behaving like this, I was glad she was there as a sort of silent mediator. But nothing would calm me down this time. I was flailing around wildly, screaming inside my head for help. In my desperation, I rang social services again, not knowing who else to call. The woman on the other end of the phone could tell I was in no state to cope and did her best to calm me down.

'Just leave your daughter with your friend for a bit,' she suggested. 'Go for a walk and a cup of coffee to get away from the situation.'

Tanya agreed to stay with the children and I almost ran outside, trying to breathe deeply and stop crying, forcing myself to try and straighten out my thoughts and work out what on earth I was going to do. Everything that was happening was driving a terrible wedge between Sarah and me. From the moment she woke up to the moment she went to bed, we were constantly on edge. If we weren't actively arguing, we were holding our anger and resentment in, or we were both just waiting for the other one to explode. It had been stupid of me to allow the success of the party to lull me into a false sense of security. Of course she would behave beautifully when everyone was paying her attention and giving her gifts, but we could hardly keep that up all the time. Maybe that psychologist had been right when he said I was the sort of parent who gave in too much.

Maybe I just wasn't being tough enough. But my instincts told me that half the time I was being too tough, going on at her all the time, driving her further into resentment.

Whatever I asked Sarah to do these days she would refuse and I kept bursting into tears as my spirits sank lower and lower. I knew a bit of uncooperativeness was normal at her age, but I somehow expected her to make more of an effort because of everything else that was happening; but that wasn't really fair on her either. All these thoughts were crowding into my head, spinning round and giving me no space to think clearly.

As I calmed down, I tried to think more positively. The one good thing was that, apart from the things she had done to Amy at school, all Sarah's destructive behaviour had been confined to the home, so at least I wasn't having to go round to other people's houses and apologise for something awful she might have done to them. It felt as if the problem was still containable, but it made me very reluctant to let her go to any of her friends' homes, even more so after the damage she had done during her sleepover. Imagine if she did that at another child's party in someone else's house! It didn't bear thinking about.

I was so grateful to Tanya for offering to take Sarah

off my hands now and then to give me a break. I didn't know how often I would have done the same for her if the roles had been reversed and Amy had been wreaking havoc on everything. But Sarah loved Tanya – in fact, it often appeared that she preferred her to me, which I could hardly blame her for, as Tanya was endlessly patient while I was in the grip of awful mood swings as I tried to control my anger and confusion at the way my family was disintegrating. While I raged around like a lunatic, Tanya was able to stay calm and reasonable. I hated the fact that I was driving my daughter further and further away from me, but how could I do anything else without it seeming to her that I was condoning her behaviour?

'I'm only going to agree to you having her,' I'd said to Tanya when she offered to have Sarah round her house again, 'if you promise to keep an eye on her every minute she's there. Because it's just not fair on you or Amy if she does something to your things while you're not looking. She might smash something that I couldn't afford to replace and I would feel terrible.'

I knew how important their material possessions were to both Tanya and Andrew, much more important than they were to Mike and me. They would care very much if something was destroyed.

'Oh, I don't mind,' she assured me. 'I'll keep an eye on her.'

'You are such a good friend,' I said, unable to keep the tears from springing into my eyes. 'I don't know how I would manage without your support. You're always there for me.'

'You help me too, don't forget,' she reminded me. 'It cuts both ways. Don't give it another thought.'

Knowing that she had a good relationship with Sarah, I was even more grateful when she would go up and talk to her at the times when I was too angry to trust myself not to say things I would regret. Tanya would reassure Sarah how much I cared for her, and at the same time try to find out why she was behaving the way she was. But even Tanya's gentle cajoling couldn't get any answers out of our stubborn little Sarah.

'She just says "I don't know" to everything,' Tanya reported back. 'Or if she doesn't like what she's hearing, she completely changes the subject, as if I'd never said anything.'

I was getting used to that trick myself and it was one of the reasons I was so close to exploding all the time. I'd be trying to find out why she had just slashed something and she would pipe up with something completely off the wall like: 'Is God real, Mummy?'

Then I discovered that £270 of Christmas Club money, which I had been about to pay to the agent, had disappeared.

Staring in horror at the empty envelope, I hoped in vain, just as I had before, that Mike had been forced to use it for some emergency or other. Because no money had gone missing for several months I knew I had let myself be careless. I had been so distracted by other things, I had dropped my guard. And I hadn't thought that Sarah knew the money was there, as I'd never seen her anywhere near the place where I hid it. But how could I be so stupid as to underestimate her after all that she had done?

My stomach churned with dread and I felt like I was going to throw up. I rang Mike at once but of course he knew nothing about it and my last ray of hope was snuffed out. If something went missing, however big or small it might be, there was really only one suspect.

Mike was home when Sarah came back from school that day, and I just didn't think I could handle another row with her. I had started to resent the fact that everything to do with Sarah's problem seemed to be down to me to deal with. It was always me who had to talk to her, and to the school and all the other experts. Mike was always too busy to come with me, or else just remained silent while I went on and on, repeating the same list of crimes and telling the same story over and over. I was fed up with him trying to pretend nothing was going on, only reacting when it was his own things that got damaged.

This time, he could take responsibility for a change.

'You deal with it,' I told him grimly.

Unable to get any more sense out of her about the money than I could, Mike became exasperated and as a punishment shredded a collection of cards he knew she had been treasuring. His reasoning was that he wanted to show her how it felt to have your things maliciously damaged or taken. I wondered if I should have thought of that, but I wasn't sure I would actually have been able to bring myself to do it.

Refusing to show any emotion as usual, Sarah stayed silent and apparently detached from the scene, making him even more furious, until eventually he lashed out and smacked her for the first time ever. Sarah was mortified. In that split second, we had crossed a boundary to another place, driven by a mixture of desperation, frustration, anger, fear and love.

It was a terrible moment. I was overwhelmed. I couldn't handle any more. I ran out the front door and went out to a friend's house. From there, I rang Tanya, knowing she would be able to cope where I couldn't, and asked her to go up and talk to Sarah for me. She could hear the desperation in my voice and didn't hesitate. When she got to the house she could see that Mike wasn't coping any better than me and took Sarah out, gently asking her what she had done with the money. A few hours later, after I'd gone to work, she came back and told Mike that Sarah had told her she'd hidden it in our bedroom, which had been stripped back at that time, ready to be decorated.

'If anyone can find out why she's doing these things,' I told one of the girls at work, 'it will be Tanya. Sarah trusts her completely, more than she does me or her father. She's like a second mum to her.'

But the money wasn't in our room. Nor was it down the drain outside, which was Sarah's next suggestion. Gentle cajoling from Tanya was no more successful at getting the truth out of Sarah than Mike's smack. There seemed to be no way into this child's head, no way of pricking her conscience and getting to the truth. But this was a lot of money to lose, and we couldn't just turn a blind eye.

In the end I told Sarah that she was going to have to stay in her room until she remembered what she had done with it. It was the holiday time, so she didn't have to go to school. I didn't lock her in the room, and she came down for meals, so she wasn't exactly a prisoner, and like any bright little girl she quickly learned how to turn the situation round so it was as much of an irritation to me as it was to her. She would sit in the bedroom, completely bored, but singing 'La, la la, la!' as if she hadn't a care in the world. About every ten minutes she would shout down to me, asking for permission to go to the toilet. Normally she has a cast-iron bladder, but I suspect she thought she could wear me down with the constant requests. Or maybe it was just her way of passing the time and stopping herself from going mad with boredom.

'Tell me what you've done with the money and we can do something nice,' I would say, and she would stare straight through me as if I hadn't spoken.

We kept this struggle up for nine whole days, and still she didn't give us any clues.

'Don't know,' she would say to every question if we insisted on an answer, with a cocky, couldn't-care-less expression on her face. 'Don't know what I've done with it.'

It was as if she was playing a game with us, which I found even more infuriating than the fact that she'd stolen the money in the first place. I could tell she was never going to relent. Despite my early misgivings about him, I had been seeing the educational psychologist connected to the school fairly regularly and I rang for advice on what to do next. I could hardly leave her in her room for ever if she really wasn't going to give in.

'You need to keep on with it,' he said. 'You need to be consistent. That is probably part of your problem, not being consistent enough.'

Part of me still thought that maybe he was right and the whole thing was my fault, brought about by my bad parenting skills. But another part could see that it was ridiculous to keep her in her room indefinitely. If she hadn't told us where the money was in nine days, I didn't think a few more days was going to make any difference and then it was going to be time to go back to school.

Having been impressed with the way the fire brigade had responded to my worries about Luke and the lighters, I called the local community police and asked if they would send a couple of officers to talk to Sarah about stealing. Two of them turned up and they were really lovely to her. They asked her where the money was too and she told them she thought it was in the kitchen; she seemed quite eager to help if she could, as she had been when Tanya had asked her, and when Mike had been looking for his computer mouse.

'I think it might be there,' she said, pointing in one direction, 'or I think it might be there.' She directed them to the other end of the room. I hoped they didn't suspect she was teasing them, because I didn't think she was. They responded to each suggestion seriously, having a look wherever she indicated the money might be. I was horrified when she pointed under a cupboard where I knew I hadn't cleaned for months.

'I've already looked there,' I jumped in, trying to distract them.

'I'll just have another look,' one of them said obligingly.

'Oh dear,' I giggled nervously. 'I'm afraid my housekeeping skills leave a lot to be desired.'

It's funny the things you worry about at moments like that. How could I still be worried about the police finding a bit of dust under my cupboards with everything else that was going wrong in my life?

In the end they left without finding the money, but they seemed to have impressed Sarah with the importance of being honest and the possible consequences of stealing, so I hoped it hadn't been a waste of their time.

17

Unseen Evil

One day, Tanya turned up on my doorstep with thick lips and black eyes.

'Oh my God, Tanya, what on earth happened?'

'Frank,' she said simply, as I led her inside.

He was still stalking and abusing her. He would go quiet for a while, leaving her alone, and then he would rage back into her life, still determined to punish her for what had happened. This time he had given her a beating.

'Hasn't Andrew noticed any of this?' I asked, gesturing at her poor battered face.

'I told him I was trying to do some stilt-walking and

fell off,' she said, giving a wry smile and grimacing at the pain.

She had to make lots of excuses to Andrew. Frank beat her up badly on more than one occasion, and once again, Tanya called me round to rescue her. She was lying on her bathroom floor, tied up as before, her hair soaked with sweat. She explained that Frank had put a carrier bag over her head and then raped her. Bad as this was, it was even worse when he assaulted her with a broom handle, leaving her barely able to walk.

'You have got to go to the doctors, at the very least,' I insisted when she told me about the broom handle.

'I can't,' she said. 'I'm too embarrassed.'

'Then you have to go to the police. I mean it, Tanya. This is intolerable. You have to put an end to it.'

'No, no,' she insisted. 'It's too dangerous. He'll kill me.'

To my horror, I then actually met Frank.

In an Internet chat room, typing away to Tanya, I was amazed when she told me that Frank was in there too, and immediately introduced me to him. I was appalled. This man was an incarnation of evil as far as I was concerned. The last thing I wanted was to have a single thing to do with him. He was poisoning Tanya's life and I didn't want him to even know I existed, let alone to start playing mind games with me.

The next time I went online, Frank was there, waiting for me. I panicked and tried to ring Tanya to tell her what he was saying, but her phone was engaged and I couldn't get through. When I did finally manage to get to her, she explained that she knew exactly what was happening because he was ringing her at the same time as chatting to me, telling her what he was saying.

'It was really freaking me out,' she said, and I had to admit it freaked me out too.

Feeling reasonably safe in my own house, I got brave and the next time Frank came online I told him what I thought of him and said he had to leave Tanya alone because I knew what he was up to and he had made her suffer enough. Whatever she had done to him as a child, she had more than paid the price and it was time for him to move on. I felt that if she wouldn't say it, then someone else had to say it on her behalf.

'*She hasn't done anything to deserve these things you're doing to her,*' I typed.

'*I hate you,*' came the reply. '*Tanya does everything you tell her to. You're a bitch . . . I hate Tanya for ruining my life . . . That's not true, I love her . . .*'

He hated her and he loved her? This was a very damaged person, I thought, damaged and dangerous.

Although I told him to leave me alone, he kept on

sending messages and something made me read them every time. I suppose I felt that I had to do what I could to protect my friend, and I was also nervous that if I didn't read the messages I might miss a warning sign and he would turn up on my doorstep and I'd be the one who ended up tied up on the bathroom floor. He started to tell me stuff about the past that Tanya had never mentioned.

'When she was fourteen she got pregnant and went into labour in school . . . She had a baby boy . . . he was all blue and she believed she had killed him.'

Tanya had never told me about a childhood pregnancy. In fact, when she'd had David, she'd given all the signs that this was her first birth. She must have blanked out the awful reality. Frank told me more and more of what Tanya had suffered as a girl. Eventually he told me it had actually been twins that Tanya had given birth to.

This is made up, I told myself. He's making up these stories to turn me against her somehow, to break us up.

As soon as I could get through, I rang and asked her about everything he had said. Horrified that he had told me her darkest secrets, she admitted that it was all true.

'I told you you'd hate me if you found out what I was really like,' she said sadly.

'I can't hate you for what happened to you when you were a kid,' I said. 'It wasn't your fault.'

But even while I was sorry with her, I was angry with Tanya for letting these things continue to happen to her. The past was the past, she could put that behind her, perhaps have counselling, and move on. If she wanted to stop what was going on in the present, she had to take control, or her whole life and everything she had built up would be destroyed.

When I got another call, asking me to go to the house and untie her yet again, I was not completely sympathetic. The door was on the latch and when I got to the bathroom I found her tied up and stark naked.

'Are you all right?' I gasped, and rushed to help her free.

'I'm so sorry,' she wept as I struggled with the knots, trying to avert my eyes. 'He just turned up unexpectedly and attacked me.'

Seeing her like this made me pity her horribly but it also made me cross. Why should my strong, determined friend be reduced to this? She had to help herself before anyone else could.

'But you must have told him you were on your own,' I said, rather testily. 'How would he have known otherwise? I can't take much more of this, Tanya, I'm serious. It's completely wrong. You have to go to the police or tell Andrew or do something.'

'Don't go to the police,' she begged.

'I'm not going to,' I assured her. 'It's not up to me. You should talk to them.'

'But I'm frightened that if I go to them everything from the past will come out. I couldn't bear everyone to know about the abuse.'

'I know, I know. But you have to talk to someone.'

'Can you get me some painkillers?' she whimpered. 'And go to Tesco and get me some bras? He's cut mine up.'

She was in such a state I had to help, but I was beginning to think she was her own worst enemy.

18

Family Therapy

Sarah was always giving me little notes, telling me she loved me, slipping them into my hand on the way to school, or leaving them for me to find around the house. She used to do it before she started behaving so strangely, and she did it much more afterwards, even though I spent so much of my time shouting at her and being angry. The fact that she was so affectionate and eager to please part of the time made it all the more bizarre that she was behaving in the other way in secret. My instincts kept telling me that it just wasn't possible that my little girl would ever do all these terrible things, but the evidence was building up and the logical side of my brain told me that I had to face the facts. It was no good giving in to my emotions and continuing to protest that my child couldn't really be this evil, that she must be innocent, that there must be some logical explanation for why she was doing all these things. The notion that I didn't even know my own children as well as I had thought I did was very hurtful.

My emotions were in tatters by now. Besides the draining effect of Sarah's activities, I had the emotional stress of Tanya's troubles to deal with as well. I was always bursting into tears, even at work, feeling like I was at the end of my tether. We had started going to family therapy, all four of us, which Sarah found very difficult. Being talked about all the time as if she wasn't there made her angry and upset, while Mike was withdrawing further and further into himself as his way of coping and Luke was getting distressed because he didn't like seeing everyone else so unhappy.

All the therapists we'd talked to had any number of suggestions as to why Sarah might feel resentful towards the world in general and her family and friends in particular. One suggested that it was because she was the youngest child; another wondered if the problem was with our marriage and the fact that we didn't spend enough quality family time together. I could see what they meant: we did all tend to go off to different rooms in the house and do our own things when we were at home, but we'd always been like that, so why would it suddenly start to affect Sarah so badly? Most families I knew, who all had televisions and computers, seemed to behave in exactly the same way as us. It might not be the idealised family life, where everyone gathers round the piano of an evening for a good old sing-song, but it seemed perfectly normal and I couldn't see why it should have such a dramatic effect on Sarah's behaviour.

'We've always been like that and she's been a perfectly happy, uncomplicated child,' I kept saying to them. 'Nothing has changed; why should she suddenly be behaving like this when nothing else is different?'

They didn't seem to be able to get their heads round what I was saying, which was very frustrating. They had their theories and they wanted to prove them.

'Ah, well,' they would say, 'children's perspectives on life change as they get older.'

'But things are bad at the moment, because of all the tension,' I reasoned, 'so if Mike and I are *forced* to spend time together artificially, instead of just getting on with our own lives, that will cause even more tension, won't it?'

Despite our reservations, we did try to change the way

we interacted as a family. It would have been mad not to try absolutely anything that was suggested if it offered even the slightest glimmer of hope. We would happily have played games of snakes and ladders all day and every day if it had solved the problem. I started by cutting down my hours at work, and took a couple of weeks off, but nothing changed. The destruction continued, so we kept on with the visits to the family therapist, just hoping that there would be some sudden blinding flash of inspiration that would explain everything. But there never was. It was beginning to feel like there would never ever be any light at the end of this tunnel.

19

Keep Out of Reach . . .

I wasn't in the mood for a visit from the family support worker that day, having just received some more shocking news. I could hear her talking and I could see her mouth moving, but I simply couldn't muster the energy to respond, too lost in my own thoughts. The woman had spent most of the time since she arrived, settled on my sofa with a cup of tea, talking about herself and her own illnesses, and when she did get on to Sarah's problems, she had suggested that perhaps I should give Sarah a pair of scissors and let her cut up one of my old T-shirts or something, in order to 'work out her feelings'. As Sarah had by that time developed something of an aversion to scissors, frightened that she would do something with them that she later wouldn't be able to remember, I didn't think that was such a good idea. I sometimes wondered if these social workers wouldn't have been happier holding workshops in drama schools than dealing with real problems in the real world. I suppose they were all becoming desperate to find something to say to me.

The reason I was so particularly distracted that evening was because Tanya had just been round to tell me that she had been going through Amy's bag after picking her up from school, sorting out her homework books, and had found five of my tranquillisers lying loose at the bottom of the bag. They were the Propranolol tablets the doctor had prescribed for my panic attacks.

This seemed a lot more serious than anything that had happened so far, apart possibly from the slicing of the Hoover wires. These were dangerous drugs for a child to be going into school with. I had no idea what I should do next and was trying to get my thoughts straight while this woman rabbited on with her daft suggestions.

Sarah was with her friend Lauren and I wanted to make some sense of what was going on in my head before she came home.

'What's wrong with you?' the woman asked, seeing I wasn't my normal talkative self.

I explained what had just happened.

'What are you going to do when Sarah gets home?' she asked, as if it was some sort of parental skills test she wanted me to pass.

Normally I would have been ranting and raving about how angry I was and what I would do this time, but now all I could say was 'I don't know'. I was beginning to sound like Sarah. It was as if we had both completely lost our way and had no idea what direction to turn in any more.

Once the woman had gone, I rang Lauren's mum, Karen, and asked her if she would talk to Sarah for me to see if she had any ideas how the tablets could have got into Amy's bag. She rang back a few minutes later to tell me that Sarah admitted it, saying she thought she had put five in there, which was exactly what Tanya had said she had found. My panic increasing, I went to look in Luke's bag, as he had now come home from school, and found four more tablets in there. When I showed them to him, I could tell he was surprised. He had no more idea how they could have got there than I did.

I felt awful because I knew I had been careless with my tablets, keeping them in an unlocked cabinet under the bathroom sink. I had never had any reason to lock them up because neither of my children had ever shown the slightest interest in touching them. I thought of all the times I had heard about how you should keep medicines out of the reach of children; why had I thought the rule didn't apply to me? Just because nothing had happened until now? What made me think that my children were any more reliable than anyone else's? Had I forgotten my own suicide attempt with my mother's tablets? I felt that this just confirmed the fact that I was a negligent mother, as some of the experts were suggesting. Not only did I run a dysfunctional family, as they had pointed out to me, where the children's father and I hardly ever spent any time in one another's company, I also left sharp blades and dangerous drugs within the reach of my children. But at the same time I knew that every family I went into had knives in open drawers and medicines in unlocked cabinets. Were all these families acting irresponsibly? Or were they just normal? It was all so confusing.

Yet another search of Sarah's bedroom turned up the empty packets that the tablets had come from. Why hadn't she thrown the evidence away? At the very least, she could have been expected to plant it elsewhere. Did she want us to know what she was up to? Or did the part of her that was doing these things just not care about being caught? There were so many questions, but absolutely no answers at all. I felt exhausted, drained physically and emotionally.

When Sarah got home I didn't rant and rave like I usually did, partly because this was now too serious for anger, and partly because I didn't feel I had the energy any longer even to raise my voice. It was almost as if she had finally defeated me. I was going to have to accept that I just couldn't control my own seven-year-old child.

'You know these are dangerous,' I said wearily, sitting on the sofa with my arm round her. 'You have to be so careful with tablets.'

'Yes,' she said solemnly, showing no signs of any guilt at all. 'I know.'

'Have you swallowed any yourself?' I asked.

'No.' She thought for a second. 'I don't know.'

I could see that she was frightened by the situation, and perhaps by the fact that I was no longer screaming. Perhaps she was scared I was about to explode again, or at the thought of what might have happened to her if she had taken any of the tablets.

By the next day, after a restless night, I had decided to ring the family therapist, even though she was always telling me I was over-anxious and kept warning me that my anxiety might be making Sarah worse. Out of all the experts I had been to see, she had been the one who had talked the most sense, even though she hadn't been able to come up with any answers.

'Why would she mess with tablets?' I asked, once I'd explained what had happened now. 'She knows they're dangerous.'

'Well, maybe it's just another thing to make you angry,' she suggested. 'Maybe that's all she wants to achieve.'

'But other children are in danger now. This is not just irritating me and her father by cutting every scrap of material in the house! Goodness knows that seemed pretty bad when it was happening, but this is much, much worse.'

There were no other solutions on offer, it seemed.

As the initial panic subsided, I found myself puzzled once more. What was Sarah's subconscious game? If her aim was to make me angry, she had been achieving that very nicely for months. I was now past anger and well into the realms of despair. I really didn't believe that Sarah would want to put Amy's or Luke's lives in any danger, even if she was angry with them both for some reason, so what was she trying to achieve? Was she trying to get Amy and Luke into trouble? Was she trying to

frighten everyone? It just didn't make sense. But sense-
less as it was, it continued happening.

A few days later, another mother at the school came
into the classroom to say she had just found a pink pill,
which had fallen out of one of the school lockers. My
heart sank; it was another one of my Propranolol tablets.
As long as the discoveries had been confined to our home
or to Tanya's home, it had felt as if perhaps we would
manage to keep our troubles at least a little private. I had
talked about the situation with a few people, like Lauren's
mum, but I hadn't gone over every gruesome detail. If
other families were going to start getting involved it was
going to be a lot harder to keep up the façade of normality. Perhaps this was what Sarah was after, a bit of
notoriety in the school. Surely not this way, though. She
had never been an attention-seeker before; why would
she want to be the centre of this sort of infamy? My big
dread now was where else these bloody tablets were
going to turn up.

A couple of days later my question was answered when
Tanya rang me on my mobile. I'd gone to town with my
mum.

'I'm so sorry, Lyndsey,' she said, 'I've just found
another tablet stuck in the mud outside the school gates.'

I was horrified, but at the same time relieved that out

of the six hundred or so people who walked in and out of those gates every day, it had been Tanya who had spotted it.

'Thank God you found it and nobody else,' I said.

Despite the urge I felt to protect Sarah's privacy, I had still been working on a policy of absolute honesty with the school, so every time something new happened I would inform the class teacher, and sometimes the head-mistress as well. Around this time they decided to separate Sarah from Amy, since the initial impetus of Sarah's attacks had seemed to be aimed towards Amy, and moved Sarah into a different class. As a result, I had a new teacher to talk to. To start with, the teachers responded very well to my concerns, working alongside me to try to help Sarah through whatever it was that was upsetting her. But gradually, as I went in to them more and more often with more and more outlandish stories of what she had done now, I could tell they were beginning to put up barriers. I was taking up a dispro-portionate amount of their time, I could see that, but what option did I have?

Like me, the teachers could see that these acts were completely out of character for the happy, well-adjusted little girl that Sarah always seemed to be in the class-room and playground. She had never been a problem child in any way, quite the opposite, and they found it as hard to believe as I did that she could be the one responsible for all these acts. But the evidence was too great to be dismissed, so they tried to think how to get to the bottom of the mystery.

I hadn't always agreed with their ideas, but I had gone along with them. Initially, when Sarah and Amy were still in the same class, the school divided the pupils up into two sets. One set was allowed to play with Sarah, the other with Amy, but they were both to stay apart from one another. I didn't argue, but the idea of this sort of segregation had made me feel very sad. However cross I was at the way Sarah was behaving, she was still my daughter. I loved her and wanted to protect her and couldn't bear to see her sad or lonely.

When I informed the school that Sarah had stolen the Christmas Club money, they said they would talk to the children generally about stealing in 'circle time'. They were very keen to help in any way they could, but for some unknown reason the teachers actually mentioned Sarah by name, saying that she had been stealing. All the children went home and told their mums the news.

'I just sat there and cried, Mummy,' she told me when she came home from school that afternoon. It ripped me up to see her like this. I thought my heart was going to break. How had it come to my little girl being alone and reviled by everyone? How had I allowed it?

I didn't say anything, clinging to the hope that she would have learned a lesson. Being publicly shamed was never going to be nice, but then it wasn't meant to be. If it discouraged her from ever stealing again, then it would have been worth it. I gave her a big cuddle and let her have another little cry.

Even after the discovery of the tablets, Tanya was still happy to have Sarah at her house to give me a break a few days later, which I thought was brilliant of her.

'Just don't leave her alone for a moment,' I begged again, dreading the thought of receiving yet another phone call.

'Don't worry,' she assured me, 'it'll be fine.'

But that same evening she was back on the phone, her voice laden with gloom.

'I'm so sorry, Lyndsey, I've just found all Amy's school work from last year,' she said. 'It's been scribbled all over and destroyed.'

'You didn't leave Sarah on her own, did you?' I wasn't sure I could handle any more bad news.

'There was about five minutes when she went upstairs and played on her own,' she admitted. I had mixed feelings; I could hardly be cross since Tanya had been doing me a favour in the first place, but how could she be so careless when she knew how dangerous Sarah was? I said nothing.

There were a few more incidents of the same kind at Tanya's house before she finally decided even she had had enough and told Sarah that she didn't want her to come back until she could behave.

'When you have stopped doing these things, Sarah,' she told her, 'you'll be very welcome to come back and play with Amy.'

That evening I noticed Sarah's attitude had hardened when she got home.

'I hate Amy,' she snapped, before I'd had a chance to say anything. 'I really hate her.'

'No, you don't,' I said, worried that she was about to finally alienate her best friend, someone who had stuck by her despite all the problems.

'Yes, I do.' I could see that she was struggling not to cry and I knew it was taking all her courage. It must have been a terrible blow to find she had been banned from the one house that had been making her welcome. I wondered if there was any chance this would be the thing that would finally make her see that she needed to mend her ways, but I didn't hold out much hope.

The school was now starting to lose patience as well,

and Sarah's new teacher was not as sympathetic as the one before had been. She made Sarah stand up in front of the whole class in order to be told off. Later that afternoon, in front of me, she told Sarah she was a 'bully' and a 'victimiser'. I was furious. I didn't see what she hoped to achieve with that sort of language and it didn't seem fair anyway.

The teachers and other experts kept giving me lectures about how I had to be stricter with Sarah, which I thought might have a grain of truth to it, but I didn't believe my lack of strictness in the past was the cause of the problem. Tanya would often be there while Sarah and I were being given these lectures, giving us moral support, but I was suspecting that she was perhaps enjoying the drama of it as well. I'd noticed she always liked to be near the centre of any excitement. I suppose a lot of people are like that, causing traffic jams by gawping at car crashes, rushing to fires with their video cameras. I suppose we all do it a bit every time we watch disasters on the television news. Tanya seemed to have enough drama in her own life, though, and I was surprised she was still so interested in what was going on in ours.

The school started a 'sanction scheme', which meant Sarah would be awarded red stickers for good behaviour and all the other things that they do for children with behavioural difficulties. Then they started a regime of checking Sarah's and Amy's belongings at regular intervals. They were reluctant to get involved as long as the incidents were occurring at home, but once the tablets starting turning up at school they began to take things more seriously. I could well understand that it wouldn't have looked good for them if one of their children had to be rushed to hospital to have its stomach pumped.

One of the sanctions Sarah had to pay was moving to the other class, away from Amy. News was spreading now and inevitably there were mothers in the new class who objected to having this 'problem child' put in with their children. Within the space of a year my daughter had gone from being a delightful model pupil whom everyone said nice things about, to being some sort of demon that other mothers wanted to protect their children from, as if she was carrying an evil virus that might be catching.

Everyone, it seemed, now felt they should be playing a part in the drama, which was being whispered about at the school gates and over coffee cups in several dozen different homes. One mother came sidling up to me one day, barely able to contain her eagerness to tell me something new.

'There's something I feel you ought to know,' she whispered conspiratorially.

'What?' I asked, guessing that whatever it was it wasn't going to be good.

'This morning in assembly the class teacher took hold of your Sarah's hand and dragged her from the centre of the row to sit at the end.'

I could just picture my poor child being humiliated in front of the whole school and I felt my anger bubbling up from just below the surface where it seemed to be all the time by then. It was the same teacher who had called Sarah a bully and victimiser, and this was the final straw. I stormed back into the school and demanded an apology for humiliating my child, as well as standing her up in the middle of the classroom in front of everyone.

'All you've done is make things worse!' I raged. 'You're making her deeply unhappy, instead of helping.'

The teacher pulled herself up to her full and considerable height, brimming with righteous indignation at the thought that I should accuse her of 'assaulting' my child, and threatened to go to her union and complain about me. I could see I was never going to get anywhere there; she had made up her mind about Sarah and nothing I was going to say would change it.

Never one to go quietly, I then wrote to the board of

governors, listing all the things that I was upset about in the school including this particular teacher, but they disagreed with me and told me that I owed the teacher an apology. By this stage, I was beginning to feel very belligerent towards anyone I felt was adding to our problems, so there was no way I was going to be apologising. I was quite convinced that they were not treating us fairly. Nothing about what was happening to us seemed to be fair and I was feeling desperate. Like a cornered animal, I was starting to fight back and it was not making me any friends, just increasing the whispers and the sideways glances.

The angrier and more ferocious I became, the more I could see people turning away, which simply fuelled the fire that was roaring away inside my head.

20

A Reputation

Perhaps if I hadn't made so much fuss, or if I hadn't been so honest and willing to tell the school everything that was going wrong with Sarah, it would have been better. If I had tried to cover things up a bit more and keep them inside the family, it might have been easier for her at school. I thought, however, that the more open and honest I was with everyone, the more likely we were to be able to find a solution to the problem between us. But my best efforts only succeeded in getting both myself and Sarah a reputation. Once you get a reputation, it is very hard to change it. Sarah was now seen as a troubled and potentially dangerous child, and I was considered a high-maintenance parent, someone who would take up a disproportionate amount of the teachers' time. But what else was I to do under the circumstances? Did they expect me to just crawl away into a corner with Sarah and hide? How would that have helped her?

When a picture was found of another girl in the class, with a message including the words 'to kill' scrawled on it in Sarah's handwriting, it seemed obvious that it was Sarah's handiwork. All around the little figure on the page was a ring of beautifully drawn daggers, pointing threateningly at her.

When I saw the picture, I recognised the writing, but not the style of the picture. In the past, I had never known Sarah draw anything except little houses with pretty gardens, happy smiling people and flowers. Never the most methodical of children, she drew her pictures quickly; they were always rushed, a bit slapdash and lacking in detail. This picture, however, although in a childish style, was perfectly symmetrical. I wasn't even aware that the girl depicted in the picture was someone Sarah had any strong feelings about at all, let alone wanted to kill.

'She's never drawn anything like this before,' I told Tanya when I saw the picture. 'If it is her work, I'm really worried now that she is mentally ill.'

I took photocopies and went to show it to a social worker, who told me it was nothing to worry about, just the sort of thing children did when they were angry with someone. I suppose they see that sort of stuff all the time, but to me it seemed a pretty shocking message, particularly if it had been written by a child who was known to have sawn through electrical wires and planted potentially lethal tablets in people's bags. I wondered if I was getting things out of proportion, losing my perspective on life.

'But it just isn't like her,' I said, wanting to scream with frustration, unable to understand why nobody was listening to me. Why were they all just brushing it away as the sort of behaviour you would expect from a child who had been poorly parented and was going through a problem period? 'Not only have I never heard Sarah ever say she wanted to kill anyone, particularly this girl, I have never known her do a neat picture before, or draw a dagger in such detail that there is a thin straight line down the centre of the blade, and in this picture there are eight of them!'

'What's she been watching on television?' the woman asked, as if she had just discovered a cure for cancer which had been staring the rest of us in the face.

'Nothing unusual,' I said defensively, assuming that she was suggesting I wasn't monitoring my children's viewing habits, and at the same time racking my brains to try to remember if we had watched any murder programmes recently, particularly any that had involved a fatal stabbing. There is, after all, hardly any shortage of them to choose from.

'So, where would she have seen pictures like this?' the woman persisted, as if talking to an imbecile.

'Well, I don't know,' I sighed, trying to cooperate. 'Her brother draws guns and things sometimes, but he's a boy; you expect that sort of thing. She's never shown any interest in weapons.'

When I talked to the family therapist, she was equally relaxed about the picture. 'It's just another thing for her to do,' she said.

'But it's not!' I seemed to be shouting all the time now and I could see that everyone was beginning to grow tired of listening, which made me want to shout even louder. They didn't quite sigh the moment they saw me coming, but their reaction wasn't far off. In a way it helped that they were so accepting that Sarah was to blame and that she had a problem: it allowed me to let them take on a role I had played before, and voice all the doubts that plagued me all the time. How?

Why? Even though there was no possible other person who could be doing these nasty acts, it still didn't add up.

But by refusing to accept what everyone was telling me, I was turning into as much of a nuisance to them as Sarah herself. I could see they were labelling me a 'difficult parent'. I didn't like it but there was no alternative. I could hardly give up trying to find out what was wrong. That simply wasn't an option.

I suspect that the teachers rather hoped I might move Sarah to another school. I had considered that, but decided against it. Since I had no idea what it was that was making her unhappy, it seemed like a mistake to start making arbitrary changes to her life. If it was something at home that was bothering her, or something inside her head, then taking her away from the friends she had known virtually all her life and starting with a whole new group of unknown people might just make everything worse. Supposing she got to her new school and didn't make any friends because she was coming in halfway through the year? What if someone started picking on her or bullying her? And her current school would probably have to make some sort of report on her, so she would arrive with a history anyway. No, I was certain it was better to keep trying to solve the problem rather than running away from it.

––––––––––

On Amy's eighth birthday Tanya decided to throw a party for her, and Sarah was invited. I was very unsure whether that was a wise idea. It hadn't been that long since Tanya had said she didn't want Sarah around her house until she could be trusted to behave; what made her think this was a safe thing to do?

'I really don't think Sarah should come,' I said. 'Just in case she does something awful.'

'Oh no,' Tanya pleaded, having been put under pressure by Amy, I suspected, 'she must come. They've been at every one of each other's birthdays ever since they were born. Please bring her. We'll both keep an eye on her.'

It was a sweet gesture considering all the trouble Sarah had caused them, and I had to agree it would have been heartbreaking for her to be left out after so many years, even if her friendship with Amy had been a bit of a roller-coaster ride. Before we left our house for the party I searched her from head to foot to make sure she wasn't hiding any tablets or knives. I looked in her pockets and her shoes and in her bag, but I didn't think to check her hands.

Betrayed

When we got to the house, I didn't take my eyes off her for a second. The party got under way and I was so pleased to see her enjoying herself with her friends again, just like in the old days. Nevertheless, I kept her under constant observation, even if I was talking to Tanya or Andrew. I feared that it had been because I wasn't always fully concentrating in the past that she had been able to get away with all the things she had. It was up to me to make sure nothing went wrong this time. Andrew was circling round with a video camera, recording everything that went on under Tanya's stern direction.

'Get a shot of the cake, Andrew. Take one of Amy and Sarah. Get a shot of the whole room and all the presents.'

Children have a wonderful way of living in the moment when they're having a good time and it was as if Sarah didn't have a care in the world. I had to admire the way in which she was able to keep her spirits up at times like this, even when so much was going wrong in her life. Sometimes I wondered if she was just being brazen and didn't care how much trouble she was bringing down on all of us, at others I was simply thankful that she wasn't withdrawing too much into a defensive shell.

Even though everything seemed to be going so well,

230

I didn't allow myself to relax. I had accepted now that I had a demon child who would do her best to outwit me if I allowed my guard to drop for even a second. All the children were sitting round a picnic table that Tanya had set up for the party. The legs can't have been properly fixed because in all the excitement it started to collapse. We all lunged forward to grab something before the whole thing hit the floor. Sarah caught her own cup and Tanya managed to catch the two cups of the children sitting either side of Sarah.

For a moment it was pandemonium, with everyone shouting and laughing as they struggled to put the table back up and get on with the party, as Andrew kept on filming. There had been no terrible damage done and the children went back to their food a few minutes later.

'Oh, Lyndsey, look,' Tanya said, staring into the cups she was holding with a horrified look on her face. 'There are tablets dissolving in these drinks.'

A familiar feeling of nausea gripped my stomach as I looked in and saw that she was right. Sarah could only have dropped them in at the moment the table had started to go because they had just begun to dissolve and were still clearly visible. How had she managed to do it without me seeing? She must have the sleight of hand of a magician. Had she deliberately sabotaged the table in some way to distract our attention at the critical moment? That was what I'd heard stage magicians did, directing their audience's eyes away from whatever movement it was they were trying to hide. How could she have developed such sophisticated skills at such a young age? Had she planned this whole thing, or had she just taken advantage of the moment?

I went completely mental, a mixture of anger and shame and panic overwhelming any good sense I might have been born with.

'Sarah, where did they come from?' I shouted. 'How did you get them into the cups without me seeing? Why did you do it? Why would you want to spoil Amy's party?'

'I don't know, I don't know, I don't know!' she was squawking, horrified that she had been caught red-handed and because she knew the happy atmosphere of the party was bound now to be over, thanks to her. 'It wasn't me, it wasn't me, it wasn't me!'

'Stop saying that!' I screamed. 'Who else could it be?'

My mind was racing. Had she managed to get to any of the other drinks? Had any of the other children drunk any of them before Tanya raised the alarm? What would it do to them if they had?

Because I worked for a telephone doctors' service, I rang it at once and asked to be put straight through to the Poisons Unit in Cardiff, thanking God that I knew such a place existed. When I got through, I told them what the pills were and asked what effect they would have on the children if they had been swallowed accidentally.

'Nothing really,' the poisons expert said, trying to calm me down. 'They might feel a bit sick but it's unlikely. It's very toxic-tasting, so they probably won't have swallowed much because they wouldn't like it.'

All the kids, however, had been infected by our panic by then and were keen to have a piece of the drama, suddenly becoming certain that they had noticed a funny taste in their drinks, and making loud retching noises as if to prove they had been poisoned.

'We have to warn the other parents,' I said to Tanya.

'Well, it's up to you,' she said kindly. 'I'm happy to keep it a secret if you prefer.'

'No, we can't do that,' I said. 'If the children have taken something, their parents have to know what's happening in case they suffer after-effects once they get home.'

I remembered how I had felt the day after swallowing my mother's tranquillisers. I don't know how Tanya thought she was going to keep it a secret when all the kids were screaming with excitement at the whole thing, convinced they only had hours to live. Did she think they were going to keep quiet about such an adventure when they got home?

It was like my worst nightmare come true. Sarah had done exactly what I had feared and outwitted all of us. Amy's party had been ruined and now everyone would know once and for all that my daughter was a danger to other children, a potential mass poisoner. What mother was even going to think of allowing her child to come and play at our house now, or would want her child near Sarah in the playground at school?

The party quickly disbanded after that and once things had settled down, Tanya and I went over everything again, trying to work out what exactly had happened and whether there was anything else we had missed.

'You know,' I said, suddenly having a terrible thought, 'Lauren's coat was in my car the whole time and Sarah could have got to it while I was driving and had my eyes on the road. Could you ring Karen and get her to check the pockets, just in case Sarah has slipped anything into them? I don't think I can face talking to anyone just at the moment.'

Tanya kindly agreed to make the call for me and Karen went away to check. To my absolute horror, she came back on the line to say that she had found a razor blade in one of the coat pockets, along with three tablets.

Things were getting worse and worse. Tanya then searched Amy's coat pockets and found three more tablets.

'Hang on a minute,' I said, unable to grasp the enormity of what was going on around me, 'I don't see how she was able to do that. She was never anywhere near Amy's coat. I'm certain I didn't give her any chance to put anything in it.'

'I wonder if David did it,' Tanya said, her voice suddenly quiet and full of dread. 'Maybe he wants to get in on the act, wanting to get Sarah into more trouble.'

'Why would he want to do that?' I was very touched that she would be willing to incriminate her own son in my daughter's crime spree to try to make me feel better, but I didn't think it was likely. 'No, I can't see it. I just have to face facts. Sarah is getting worse.'

As I was leaving with Sarah, Tanya mentioned she might sit down with Andrew to watch his videoing handiwork, to enjoy the good bits of the party again and to see if they could spot any clues as to how Sarah had managed to pull off her trick. When she called later that evening I already knew she was going to confirm my worst fears.

'Did you check her hands before she came out?' she asked when I picked up the phone.

'No,' I said, feeling a terrible premonition of what was coming. 'I don't think I did.'

'We've looked at the video. Sarah's keeping her fists clenched the whole time up until the table collapsed and there were all those distractions. The tablets must have been in her hands all the time.'

I still couldn't believe that it was possible Sarah had been quick enough to drop tablets into two different glasses without me noticing when I was watching her all the time, apart from the few seconds when the table was collapsing. But Tanya put Andrew on the phone and he appeared to be as convinced as she was. It seemed I truly did have a daughter who was a cross between the devil and a genius.

The next day at school, the children were all eager to spread the news of their narrow escape from poisoning by Amy's wicked friend, shouting about how Sarah had tried to murder them all. I couldn't blame them, although I might have wanted to murder them all myself at that moment. With each retelling, Amy's birthday party was becoming more lurid and terrifying, until it was beginning to sound worthy of its own television documentary.

Some of the mothers were very sensible and told their kids not to be silly and that they had never been in any danger of being murdered, but others were carried away with the drama themselves and fed their children's anxieties with their own. All the resentments from the mothers of the class that Sarah had been moved to were rekindled. Why, they wanted to know, did they have to have the devil child moved in to share a classroom with their little angels? What if she tried to kill them? The school remained firm in their decision and refused to bow to the pressure for a witch-hunt, for which I was grateful.

———

In the moments when I wasn't telling Sarah off after some new discovery, she often still managed to be the same loving child she had been before the whole nightmare began. She would still write me little notes, telling me she loved me, or would suddenly throw her arms around me for a spontaneous hug. I had to remember that she was only seven years old. She needed the reassurance that her mother still loved her unconditionally, no matter what she had done.

One of these sudden hugs, when she launched herself at me unexpectedly, wanting to tell me how much she loved me, took me by surprise. I had a cigarette in my hand and didn't have enough time get it out of the way of her face. The burning end jabbed into the middle of Sarah's forehead, making her jump back with a scream of shock. I screamed too – it's always ghastly when you accidentally hurt one of your own children and it seemed doubly awful that I had done it at a moment when all she wanted to do was show affection. It only added to my growing suspicions that I might be as bad a mother as some of the experts were suggesting. The burn mark was very noticeable, like a bullet hole in the centre of Sarah's head, and I couldn't think of any way to help her cover it up, so the next day, when I went into school to collect her, I explained to the teacher what had happened.

'I hope you don't think I did that on purpose,' I laughed, trying to sound jocular about it and probably just sounding dementedly guilty. I didn't want them to get the idea that there was someone stubbing out cigarettes on my poor troubled daughter, in case they jumped on that as the obvious reason for all her behavioural problems. The teacher looked a bit stony, but I knew she was pretty fed up with me by then anyway. I didn't know that she had already asked Sarah how she got the burn. I suppose if I had been her, it might just have crossed my mind that a guilty mother would have primed her daughter to back her up with the same story.

I understand that they have to keep their eyes open for children who might be being abused, and I also understand that all the mystery that surrounded Sarah's behaviour must have seemed a bit suspicious.

All the understanding in the world, though, didn't stop me from feeling outraged that anyone would suspect us of such a thing.

There had been another occasion where Sarah had gone into school with a massive bruise on her leg after falling off a chair in the conservatory on to the pedal of a bike. Mike had taken her into the classroom the next day on that occasion, because I'd got fed up with always being the one to have to face them, and the teacher had asked him about the bruise in front of all the other parents, which didn't seem very diplomatic. I was glad to think that they were keeping an eye on things like that, but I was cross they had done it in front of everyone else, particularly since I was sure tongues were already wagging all around us. People do tend to believe that there is no smoke without fire, and often they're right. I appreciate that it's difficult for teachers when they are duty-bound to look out for child abuse all the time, but I thought on that occasion it might have been more appropriate for them to have taken Mike to one side to chat to him.

The nightmare just kept on. Tablets kept turning up in different places and I simply couldn't understand how Sarah was getting hold of so many. I'd locked them up long ago. I could only assume she must have built up a store of them somewhere, but where was it hidden? I searched in all the usual places, and a few more besides, but came up with nothing. With each new discovery, I told myself that this must be the last of her supply, but it never seemed to be.

I keep a full water jug in the kitchen for the children to drink out of whenever they're thirsty and on one occasion I found half a dozen tablets just beginning to dissolve in it. Another day I picked up a pint glass of squash that Luke had left on the side. I don't usually drink squash but I was thirsty and I drained it down to the bottom; as I glanced into the dregs I saw the ominously familiar pink debris swilling around. These tablets never really dissolved completely, always leaving a telltale residue. I knew Luke's glass had been standing there quite a while so I had no idea, as usual, when Sarah would have slipped the tablets into it. Yet again, she had been too cunning for me to catch her. I was especially worried about Luke in these situations because he is asthmatic and drugs like these could have caused him to suffer a more serious reaction than most children.

One day Sarah and I went out to lunch with a friend at a carvery and I left Sarah to look after my handbag at the table while I went up and got our food. It wasn't until the next day that I discovered the Seroxat tablets I was taking for depression had disappeared from my bag. I couldn't be certain that it had happened in the restaurant, but I couldn't think of any other moment when she could possibly have got to the bag without me seeing. I dreaded having to tell the school yet again, knowing they would think I had been incredibly negligent in leaving the bag within Sarah's reach. Because it had been in a public place and there had been someone else at the table, I had thought it was safe. Would I never learn?

'You really shouldn't have left your tablets in your bag,' the teacher lectured when I owned up. 'You shouldn't be leaving Sarah unattended at any time.'

'How many times do I have to tell you,' I said, unable to hide my exasperation, 'she is not left unattended. She used to be. I used to be upstairs in bed and she would be happily downstairs watching telly with Luke, but that all had to stop. She is never left to roam the house on her own. The poor girl can't even go to the toilet without being cross-examined about where she's going and what's she up to.'

It didn't matter how much I protested, the lecturing

went on and on. I had tears running down my cheeks, but the teacher just kept on hectoring me about my shortcomings as a parent.

'You can judge me as much as you like,' I snapped eventually. 'You can criticise me as a parent and say it's all my fault, but I am doing my bloody best. I am getting as much help as I can. I am telling you everything that is going on. I cannot do any more.'

'I'm not judging you,' she protested, trying to back-pedal.

'You bloody well are and I've had enough of it.'

I felt bad because I knew that, up to a point, she was right: it had been negligent to leave Sarah with the bag for those few seconds. But there was still a part of me that trusted her and was unable to believe that she really was turning into this appalling little girl. I was angry to think that she had betrayed my trust yet again. She had made a fool of me when I was spending almost every hour of my days trying to think of ways to protect her.

21

Exploring the Dark

The world had become a much darker and more frightening place for me. Once, it had been fairly straightforward. There were good times and bad times, rows and fallings-out along with strong relationships and mutual support. Gradually, though, everything had been changing and I was beginning to think that I'd never understood life at all. Things that I'd only heard of in horror stories or seen in the movies began to seem like normal, everyday existence. Things I'd never imagined could happen to me, or to people I know, had begun to invade my consciousness. With every step down the path, events I would once have gasped at became entirely credible.

While my draining and desperately worrying family problems grew ever worse, my best friend was confiding more about her life than I thought was possible. A lifelong victim of abuse, she was proof that once you were put on that dreadful road, it was very, very hard to get off it. The shadows of her past pursued her; Frank, her childhood friend, had not stopped victimising and punishing her for whatever she had done to him years before. Tanya and I spent many hours together as she told me, very slowly and very gradually, the full extent of what had happened to her in the past. And in the Internet chat rooms, Frank was still waiting to tell me the things she wouldn't.

The childhood abuse that Tanya suffered at the hands of her father was much worse than she had first indicated. Gradually and tentatively she told me that her mother had known about the abuse. Not only had she condoned it, she had stood by and watched.

'Tanya, are you sure?' I gasped. I couldn't imagine any mother who would be able to do such a thing. I had met Tanya's mother – we had shared babysitting duties together. I would never have guessed in a million years she could be capable of such monstrosity. 'Could you have dreamed it?'

'I don't think so,' Tanya said mournfully. 'I am sure she was there. I remember it clearly. I thought she would help me. But she didn't.'

She said she remembered being told to wear a certain dress and that she had seen photos that were in Frank's possession – they showed her mum in the room as she was being abused.

'I believe they knew everything,' she said. 'In fact, I think they were paid to let others abuse me.'

It was such a dreadful thing to suspect about your own parents, I hardly knew what to say to her.

'How can you still see them? How can you trust them with your own children?'

Just as she had all that time ago, when I'd first asked her the same question, she looked astonished and child-like. 'You don't think they'd do the same to my kids, do you?'

I didn't know what to say any more. In my heart, I didn't think they would because I found it so hard to reconcile the people I knew with the depraved pair Tanya described. But I also thought that if Tanya had the slightest doubts, it was amazing that she allowed her children to stay overnight at their grandparents' house.

The revelations gradually became more intense. I already knew now that Tanya had suffered long-term abuse that had led to a pregnancy, and that she was still enduring horrific encounters with Frank, a man she seemed locked into a bizarre and masochistic relationship with. The things he was doing to her were so dreadful that it seemed to me that they could only happen with some kind of collaboration with Tanya herself. It was mysterious and strange, as well as terrible.

The situation became worse and worse. Frank kept coming to the house and attacking her, and on one occasion he brought a woman with him, and she also attacked Tanya. She started to cry as she told me, confessing that she was worried because she had actually enjoyed the role the woman played in the proceedings and she was afraid she might be a lesbian. I spent ages trying to explain that I was sure it was just a physical reaction and that she shouldn't feel guilty about it, although I don't know what made me think I was an expert on the subject. I hated to see her punish herself so badly, when I could see clearly that she was a victim who deserved no blame at all.

'It's them with the problem, not you!' I said furiously. 'You mustn't blame yourself.'

But Tanya was so full of guilt, it was impossible to make her acknowledge that she wasn't to take responsibility for what was happening to her.

'I asked for it,' she wailed. 'I deserve it.'

After the abuse she suffered as a young child, and the awful experience that Frank had revealed, when she'd gone into labour at school, Tanya had done what many victims before her had done. She had used sex as a way to control her life, even while it took her control away.

She explained how she became the school 'bike', willing to sleep with any boy who asked. Her self-respect was non-existent and she didn't think she was worth anything at all. Once she started talking, it all poured out. She told me dreadful, intense stories of rape and violence that sounded like something from a Stephen King novel. She had been pregnant twice more after losing the twins, first with a stillborn child, whose grave she once took me to, and then, when she was sixteen and as a result of Frank raping her, she was forced to give away her second child, a little boy. Only many years later did she discover that he had been given to an aunt and uncle of hers and that she had been told it was her new cousin. By the time she found out the truth, the boy was married with a baby.

'So I am actually a grandmother,' she said proudly, but a little sadly.

When she told me of these terrible experiences, she would be racked with sobs, her whole body trembling, or hyperventilating to the point of almost passing out. I wasn't surprised at the extent of her physical reaction. These were events I never dared think could actually happen to people I knew. With all the weird things that were happening around Sarah in my own house, I now knew only too well how unexplainable and unbelievable events can happen in the most normal and unexpected of places.

When she sat in front of me, hysterical with grief and despair, I felt so sorry for her. I pitied her terribly and couldn't imagine how she had managed to live a normal life at all after such terrible experiences. It made me count my own blessings, and feel deeply thankful that I had never had to suffer in the same way. Tanya had attracted the most loathsome sort of people in the world and I was grateful I had never had to meet such types. It was a case of 'There but for the grace of God go I'.

Sometimes I cried with her. At other times, the stories were so chilling and shocking – such as the deaths of her babies – that I couldn't shed a tear. I was frozen to the core by what she was telling me.

I couldn't imagine how she could live with so many painful memories inside her head.

Some things that Frank told me about her in the

chat room she would deny when I asked her and become very angry, slamming the phone down on me as if I was making it up just to embarrass her. I was increasingly frightened that he would come round the house and wished I could tell Mike what was going on, but Tanya had made me give her my word, over and over again, never to tell her terrible secrets to another living soul.

The more she told me the more I realised I was completely out of my depth, and that my friend had been appallingly damaged by the events of her childhood and that she needed serious help. She had lived for so many years in a world I couldn't understand, filled with terrible people who did terrible things, that she had lost all sense of what she could and couldn't do to take control of her own destiny. She didn't seem to be able to grasp the fact that she didn't have to allow people to abuse her any more. She told me that, even now she was an adult, her father would often force her to have sex with him from time to time, which filled me with pity and revulsion. She was utterly unable to break free.

I might have been able to listen and be supportive, but I didn't know what else to say to her. At the same time I found myself becoming exasperated by the way she dwelt on the past as if deliberately torturing herself with the painful memories. She would go over and over things, each time making them more dramatic than the last time. I couldn't help losing patience at times and I felt guilty that I wasn't being completely sympathetic. Sometimes I even got cross and told her not to behave so stupidly. She had to put a stop to it all, and seek help. I wanted to seek help for her myself, but I had to respect her wishes and keep it a secret, as she had asked me to.

With everything else that was going on in my life, I went through a stage when I found it hard to be patient with all Tanya's traumas, and I tried to discourage her from coming up to the house quite so much when the kids were at school, to give myself a little bit more space to think and try to work out everything that was happening in my life.

'You're worried about having me around your kids, aren't you?' she said when I tried to put her off again. 'You're afraid I might abuse them after everything that has happened to me, aren't you? They say abusers have always been abused themselves and you think that's me!'

I was horrified that she would think such a thing, but I could see how she might come to that conclusion. Someone who had been as badly damaged as she had as a child was bound to be extra sensitive. It hadn't occurred to me for a second that she would ever do anything to harm the children, I knew exactly how much she loved them and they loved her in return, and so I started making an extra effort to invite her round when they were there, just to show her how much I trusted her.

I became so involved with her life that when she finally agreed to go to therapy sessions, I ended up going along with her. She would talk to her counsellor and it seemed to help, but there was a lot she didn't tell. She never mentioned the abuse by her father, for example.

'Why don't you tell her about your dad?' I asked her.

'I can't. You tell her,' Tanya said, as if she was a small child, unable to talk for herself.

'I can't,' I said. 'This isn't my life – it's yours. You need the professional help and you must confide in her.'

But Tanya found it impossible to tell her counsellor the full extent of what she had suffered.

'Promise me one thing,' the woman said to me, when we had a moment alone one day. 'Don't let Tanya become the only thing in your life. Continue to have other friends and continue to work, or she'll drag you into her world with her.'

'All right,' I said, a little surprised. I had always worried that I had been dragging Tanya into *my* world, burdening her with my worries about Sarah, but then this woman didn't know anything about all that. 'But she is my friend; I have to do whatever I can to help her.'

The woman smiled understandingly and nodded, and I had a feeling there was something she wasn't telling me.

22

The Holiday

I had only ever been abroad once, on a girls-only holiday to Magaluf, during which I missed Mike and the kids so much, I squandered all my money on phone calls home (well, I squandered some of it on cigarettes as well, if the truth be known). In November of 2003, when the skies were as grey as my mood, I decided it would be a good idea for us to go on a family holiday to get a bit of winter sun in Tenerife. I thought it would do us good to get away from the English weather, and away from the house which had become like a prison to all of us. It would mean taking the children out of school for a week, but, not surprisingly, the school didn't put up any sort of protest at all! I dare say they would have been happy to see the back of us once and for all.

'Holiday, Mrs Harris? Certainly. Have you considered the advantages of emigration?'

Mike never responds very well to surprises. He doesn't like doing anything on the spur of the moment. He never has and I doubt if now he ever will. He'd also never flown before and I could tell he was extremely nervous at the idea. I could see I should have given him more time to get used to the plan, but I hadn't and now I was in a hurry. Having had my flash of inspiration, I just couldn't wait a moment longer than I had to before jetting off to a warm beach. I told him I was going to order him a passport anyway, and he could decide when it arrived if he wanted to come or not.

I hoped Mike would decide to come. I wanted him to be with us, and so did the children, but he was so reluctant that I didn't hold out much hope. When Mike makes up his mind about something, it's hard to change it. I knew I could force him to do it if I really wanted to, but I didn't want him to come under those conditions. Our relationship needed some attention, I thought, and it would help us to spend some quality time together away from all the hassles and niggles of home and work.

His new passport arrived on the Friday, but on the

following Monday, when Mike went to look for it, he couldn't find it. For a second I wondered if he had hidden it just to get out of the trip, but I could see from his re-action that he hadn't. Mike has always been a rotten liar. So it had to be the usual suspect. I immediately started giving her the third degree.

'Have you taken Dad's passport?' I demanded.

A wary look. 'I don't know.'

'You must know. Have you taken it?'

'Yes, all right, I took it.'

'Right. So then – where have you put it?'

'I don't know.'

'Come on, Sarah,' I coaxed, suppressing my rising exasperation. 'If we can find it, maybe next year we can all go to Disneyland Paris together.'

'I don't know,' she muttered stubbornly, making me want to scream.

So, once again, we searched her room. There it was, under her bed, all the pages ripped and scribbled on, just like Amy's schoolwork and the Christmas Club cheques. It looked as if she had tried to prise Mike's photo out as well, but had given up when it wouldn't come cleanly. It was a week before we were due to go, so I rang the Passport Office and explained what had happened. I asked if Mike would still be able to use it but they told me that a damaged passport wouldn't be acceptable.

Mike said then that he would have come if he could have, but now of course Sarah had made it impossible. That seemed a bit convenient to me, but I wasn't about to start another row.

I was not going to let this stop me getting my holiday. I was determined to take the children away for a week, just to try and break the cycle of all the trouble at home and at school, to get some perspective and maybe have a chance to think about things from a different angle. Apart from anything else, Luke deserved a reward for being such a long-suffering and patient brother and son.

The timing of the holiday was not good for Tanya, who had just discovered she was pregnant again and wanted me to be there to help her sort it out.

'I don't know who the father is,' she wept as she told me. 'It could be Andrew's or Frank's. I'll have to get rid of it.'

She was going to have the termination while we were away, and I really wanted to be there for her as I was sure it would be a terrible experience, but I felt my first duty was to the children. If I told them the holiday was cancelled because of Tanya, without being able to tell them the full story, they would be quite justified in thinking I wasn't putting them first. Tanya was a grown-up, I told myself, who was partly responsible for the state she was in and would therefore have to look after herself for a while, until I got back. I told her she could ring me at any time because I would have my phone with me, and we set off on my first foreign family holiday.

I'm sure that Mike regretted being left behind as he waved us all off at the airport and I hoped that it would be easier next time to persuade him to come with us.

One of my main problems had been finding enough clothes to pack, since Sarah had cut up virtually everything I owned at one time or another. Tanya was very sweet and lent me a heap of her things. I was terrified that Sarah would do something to them while we were away, and was constantly checking them and hiding them away in the hope she would forget they were there.

Arriving in the sun on a holiday island was like magic. The moment we stepped off the plane into the warmth of Tenerife, all of our troubles back in England seemed a million miles away. The self-catering apartment I'd booked was a little bit more of a dive than I had been expecting, but the kids didn't care; they just wanted to spend the whole day by the pool anyway. Luke found it particularly amusing that I was petrified of the huge cockroach that appeared to live permanently in the kitchen.

We went on a number of excursions. One was to a nearby theme park where they did things like a seal show and a parrot show, and another was to an equestrian event and barbecue in a castle. One evening Sarah stood up and sang a Busted number in a karaoke bar in front of quite a big crowd and I thought I was going to burst with pride. The next day she saw one or two people pointing her out – 'There's that little girl who sang last night' – and the attention made her glow. We had a really fabulous time, and for a while it was a welcome glimpse of the family life we should be enjoying.

Tanya called me all the time. She had had her termination.

'I want my baby,' she wept, once there was no chance of changing her mind. 'I wish I hadn't done it.'

I felt so sorry for her, and wished I could be there to comfort her. I felt quite guilty to be enjoying myself so much with Sarah and Luke while my friend was having to go through so much pain alone. Then, in a later call, she told me she had a confession to make.

Oh my God, I thought, what else could there possibly be?

'I'm afraid I've been up to the school,' she said. 'I had

to tell them that I didn't realise just how worried I was about Amy's safety until Sarah wasn't there. I'm so sorry. I feel so bad about it.'

My heart sank, but I could understand how it might happen. Given a few days to think clearly, she had realised what a constant worry it was to have Sarah near to Amy. I probably would have felt the same if the boot had been on the other foot. In fact, I probably would have said something sooner, like the other complaining mothers.

I was also worried about Mike, left at home all on his own, and at first rang him every day. I could tell from his tone, though, that he'd got over his sadness by the time he got back from the airport and had settled into a comfortable bachelor routine in the house on his own. I decided not to worry about Mike, much as we all wished he was there to share our good time, but relaxed and got on with enjoying myself. The kids missed him and were as determined as I was to make sure that next time he would come with us, whether he liked it or not.

There was no safe in the apartment, so I hid the passports and tickets in a book. When I couldn't find them a few days later, I knew immediately that I wasn't going to be able to escape my nightmare just by getting on a plane. I was furious with Sarah for ruining such a great holiday for all of us, and I was also desperate because I had no idea what to do in a foreign country with no papers. I could understand that she might think that she could prolong our holiday by hiding them, but knowing that didn't make me any less panic-stricken. It was scary enough being abroad on my own with the children, never mind being stranded with no papers. Who the hell should I go to for help? Who would advise me? What should I do? Would I have enough money to do what-ever I had to do to get us home?

I became hysterical, yelling at Sarah to tell me what she'd done with them, as if that had ever done any good in the past.

She yelled back, 'I don't know what I've done with them!'

Poor Luke looked like he was about to have a nervous breakdown. If there is one thing a naturally anxious child doesn't need it is a panicking parent.

I hoped she had hidden them in the apartment some-where, because if she hadn't, then they could be any-where by now. I just kept searching and searching, becoming angrier and more frantic with every failed attempt.

The moment I found them in the book, I remembered putting them there. The realisation that I had not only made a complete fool of myself, but also falsely accused Sarah made me feel even worse than I had when I'd thought they were lost. Relieved as I was to find them, I could hardly bear to think how I must have made Sarah feel. I'd jumped to a conclusion that she was guilty, just as everyone kept doing back home. Of course, she must be responsible for some of the things that were going on because there was no other explanation for most of them, but this incident reawakened the fear in me that she was turning into everyone's scapegoat.

If her own mother was jumping to conclusions about her, how could we not expect other people to do the same? The drawing with the daggers, for instance, that could have been done by anyone who disliked the girl in the picture. The tablets in Amy's coat pocket when I knew that Sarah had gone nowhere near the coat – it could have been David, as Tanya had suggested. Why did I automatically assume it was Sarah? And then there was that razor blade in Lauren's coat pocket. How had she managed to hold it in a clenched fist without cutting herself? But who else would have done such a thing?

I went round in circles. It was impossible to tell what was true and what was false. When was Sarah being honest and when was she lying? She had admitted so many of the crimes I'd accused her of – but then, she'd immediately confessed to taking the passports when she hadn't. I was sure of nothing. The fact that I had just misjudged her so spectacularly brought back all my fears that she was being falsely accused. I was flooded with sadness because I didn't know what to do about it.

'Oh, Sarah, I'm really, really sorry,' was all I could say, over and over again.

As I grasped for some sort of excuse, I explained how people were bound to jump to conclusions about her because of the other things she'd done. I tried to tell her that if she could just stop her activities, people would not suspect her of being guilty of the things that she hadn't done – but I could see I was losing her interest. The poor girl did not deserve yet another lecture when, this time, she hadn't done anything wrong. I was desperate to get us back into the high holiday spirits we had been in before I lost all sense of proportion.

Children are wonderfully forgiving creatures some-times. Within a few minutes, Sarah had apparently for-gotten the whole incident and had gone back to enjoying the holiday with no sulking, no recrimination or resent-ment. I loved her so much at that moment and I was so grateful to her for showing me such mercy.

As we returned home, we all felt really refreshed and happy. I hoped that maybe getting away would have had the desired effect on Sarah and that we could put the terrible past year behind us and go back to being a normal happy family. I was determined that it wouldn't be too long before we went on holiday again, and next time I wanted to make sure Mike came too. Knowing that he just couldn't handle anything too spur-of-the-moment, I decided to book the next one a year in advance, so he wouldn't have any excuse for not coming with us.

A few days after we got back, I checked through all the clothes Tanya had lent me to make sure Sarah hadn't got to them while I was sleeping or in the bathroom or just looking the other way at the crucial moment, and gave them back to her, pleased to report that all was well. Tanya took them out to her car, but brought them back a few minutes later to show me that there were all sorts of little nicks in them that I hadn't noticed. I felt so bad. How could I have missed them? I'd always known that I was careless about these sorts of things, and not nearly as observant or methodical as Tanya, but I genuinely thought I had gone over every garment with a fine-tooth comb.

I began to wonder if the stress I had been living under for nearly a whole year was having an effect on my mind, making me unable to notice things that I didn't want to see. In a way, it was a mercy, but it was embarrassing when Tanya had been kind enough to lend me clothes that were now all ruined. As always, she was incredibly understanding and assured me I didn't have to think about replacing anything, but I knew I would have to do something as soon as I could afford it.

It was so disappointing. The holiday seemed to have been a turning point. We had had a wonderful time and I had thought Sarah was back to her normal self. But all along, it was an illusion. She had been continuing her campaign of destruction in secret. I felt I had been betrayed again, and made to look stupid and deluded. The nightmare had resumed.

23

Exclusion

Almost as soon as we got back home, I received a call from the headmistress to say that Sarah wasn't allowed to go back because the school were worried about the safety of the other children. I suppose that they had to react to Tanya's concerns; if something had happened to Amy after Tanya had been in to talk to them, they wouldn't have had a leg to stand on. I was so despondent to think that after all my struggles it had come to this, but it had a sort of terrible inevitability about it. There was bound to come a time when they would have to respond to the pressures of the other parents.

'Before she can come back, we need to be able to arrange

for Sarah to be supervised at all times,' the headmistress
went on, 'and that may take a little time to organise.'

To allow Sarah to return, they needed to have a full-
time carer with her every moment that she was with
them on school premises, just to watch her and make
sure she didn't do anything to endanger the other children. The problem was, as it always is in these situations,
funding. The headmistress explained that they had to
find a way to pay an extra salary, which meant applying
to the local education authority (LEA) as they didn't
have any spare money in their own budget. The school
wasn't actually the one for our catchment area, so they
had no legal obligation to take Sarah unless the LEA was
willing to pay the extra money. If not, the LEA would
move her to another school, which might now be hard
to do when she had a record for being so disruptive. I
could just imagine how the parents at the new school
would rally round to stop Sarah from coming into class
with their children once they heard the rumours about
her past.

Things were now getting completely out of my control. The school called a meeting to discuss Sarah and
what was going to happen. They said we didn't need to
attend, but there was no way I was going to allow them
to talk about Sarah behind my back, so Mike and I went

to put on a united front. Their hearts must have sunk when they realised they weren't going to be able to put me off. When we got there, there were seventeen professionals in the room, all discussing what to do about one little girl, our 'problem child'.

The teacher I had told about the mark on Sarah's forehead made a point of asking about it again in front of everyone, just when the whole room had fallen quiet, in a voice that suggested she wanted everyone to note.

'Tell us, Mrs Harris, how did Sarah get that cigarette burn on her face?'

'I've already told you,' I replied, feeling myself flushing with anger and aware that the more I protested that it was an accident, the more it was going to look as if I'd done it deliberately and was trying to cover my tracks. But I just couldn't stop myself from blundering on in my anger. 'If I was going to do it on purpose I certainly wouldn't have done it anywhere you could see it!'

There was an uncomfortable pause as everyone took in without a hint of a smile what was meant to be a sarcastic remark. They were right of course; this was not a laughing matter in any way. Why couldn't I just learn to keep my mouth shut?

'Has anyone in your family got a history of mental illness?' the headmistress chimed in at one point.

'I do suffer depression,' I said cautiously, fearing a trap. Were they suggesting I was mad?

'I was referring to your mother,' she said, peering at me disapprovingly over her glasses.

I assumed she was talking about the nervous breakdown Mum had had while I was a child, which didn't seem relevant to Sarah who hadn't even been born at that time.

'She has been on medication and she went into hospital once,' I snapped. 'What's that got to do with anything?'

It was obvious they were implying that Sarah had inherited mental health problems – or maybe they were referring to me and what I might have inherited. I couldn't be sure and I didn't think it would be wise to ask.

'Can we just interrupt?' It was one of the people from the Child and Adolescent Mental Health Team. 'Sarah is not mentally ill. There's no point going down that route.'

I could have hugged him then and there for that, but I forced myself to say nothing.

The educational psychologist remained silent and the teachers all averted their eyes. There was no way of telling what was really going through their minds now. Instead, they talked and they talked and they talked, but none of them had any more idea of what Sarah's problem was, or how she should deal with it than Mike or me. Everyone agreed that they had never come across a case like it, which amazed me when I thought about how many combined years of experience of working with children there were sitting in that room that day. It's never a good idea to have something unusual wrong with you.

'You can say something if you like,' someone said to Mike at one stage. Perhaps they thought that I was talking too much and not giving him a chance. I dare say they had him down as a henpecked husband. But, as usual, Mike didn't have anything he wanted to add to the proceedings, and I guessed that they were drawing a few more negative conclusions about our relationship from that. Perhaps they suspected that he was too frightened to speak up while his monster of a wife was in the room. Or perhaps he disagreed with everything I said.

Although it would have been nice if Mike had been more proactive, in a way he was right, there really wasn't anything else to say. Not that I was going to let that stop me.

'You all sit here and say how terrible the situation is,' I piped up as the proceedings drew to a close, 'but you don't have to live with it. At the end of the day, we love

Sarah and we want what's best for her. You can all go home after work and get away from the problem, but we can't.'

I was quite proud of myself because I managed to give the whole speech without getting too emotional or aggressive. But even though I thought I had coped quite well with the meeting, I could tell they were getting fed up with me. Whereas in the beginning they had reacted well every time I went in or called, now they were not returning my phone calls or letters and I could see the looks on their faces whenever they saw me approaching. They were coming to the conclusion that I was the problem rather than Sarah, but they hadn't quite worked out what it was that I was doing.

Could they be right? Was my attitude making this whole situation worse? Should I just leave everyone to get on with their jobs?

I couldn't do that. It would feel like throwing my daughter to the lions and I could never do that. I had to continue fighting her corner as best I could, however badly it reflected on me.

I was still worried that it might be my parenting skills that were causing Sarah to behave so strangely, but none of the things that the experts were telling me I was doing wrong seemed serious enough to throw a child so completely off the rails. Lots of mothers were inconsistent and over-anxious and their children didn't end up sneaking about the place trying to poison and electrocute people and cutting up their possessions.

We had no choice but to go away from that meeting leaving them to decide Sarah's fate. While the various authorities thrashed out a way to finance a carer in meetings behind closed doors, Sarah would have to stay at home with me. In reality, it meant that her education ground to a complete halt. They sent homework to us, but trying to get Sarah to do it caused more arguments between us.

'I'm not doing it,' she would pout whenever I brought the subject up. 'I hate you.'

On the one hand, I was anxious that she was falling behind her peer group, but on the other I could see that finding the motivation to do the work without any of the stimulus of having her friends or teachers around her was almost impossible. I doubted if I would have reacted any differently at her age. It was hard on both of us being forced together all the time in the atmosphere of mistrust that had haunted us for so long.

I was still working nights, partly because we needed the money and partly because I needed to get out of the house for at least a few hours in every twenty-four. Tanya was wonderful at coming round to look after Sarah during the day when I was sleeping. She would sit and chat to her, cuddle her, brush her hair, take her out. I was more relieved than I could say that they had such a brilliant relationship; it took just a little of the pressure off me.

I admired Tanya so much for the way she was able to be so kind and patient with my children and me when she had been and was going through so many terrible experiences herself. I tried to repay her by being as good a friend as possible when she needed it, but sometimes it was difficult.

One day she told me a worse story than I had heard her tell for a long time. Frank had been back, but this time he had brought some friends. They had all attacked her, and she had been raped. It was another act of vile cruelty among so many others.

I tried to be sympathetic but it took all my self-control not to flare up with anger. I couldn't think why it was making me angry that Tanya refused to sort this problem out but it was. I couldn't understand how she could keep colluding in being Frank's victim when she had a lovely home and a wonderful family she loved. She just seemed to refuse to help herself. Listening to her terrible troubles was beginning to make me feel torn between my need to support her and my deep sense of frustration that she absolutely refused to do anything that might stop these things happening. It began to make me think that I would never be able to help her out of the darkness and that, perhaps, in some strange way, she didn't want me to.

———————

Tanya and Andrew and the kids came to us on Christmas Eve that year, as they normally did. It had become a ritual in both families and we all looked forward to it, particularly the kids. That was what made it all the more surprising that Sarah used the occasion to put yet another tablet in Tanya's drink. Luckily Tanya spotted it before she drank it because, as usual, Sarah's sleight of hand had been too fast for any of us to see her doing it. Thank God it wouldn't have done Tanya much harm even if she had swallowed it, since they were tablets she sometimes took herself anyway, but that wasn't really the point. It was the idea that it was being administered so slyly that was spooky, and by a seven-year-old. If she could do it with these tablets, what would happen if she managed to get hold of something really dangerous? In a few years' time, she could be offered illegal drugs by older kids – what if she was still slipping things into people's drinks then? The possible consequences were too ghastly even to think about.

I had so hoped that nothing like this would ever happen again. Each time I was lulled into a false sense of hope by Sarah behaving for a while, and each time I was disappointed all over again. The discovery caused the usual overreaction from me, and a sad sort of acceptance from Sarah. She seemed as disappointed as the rest of us that she had ruined Christmas Eve. I sent her up to her room, feeling as if my heart was going to break, and she went with her head down and her hair covering her face, hardly making any protest at all. Our Christmas high spirits had vanished and we were back inside our living nightmare.

'I wouldn't give her any presents tomorrow if I were you,' Tanya said, 'to teach her a lesson until she behaves.'

'I don't think I could do that,' I said. I couldn't help feeling that in some perverse way Sarah was suffering enough already. 'I couldn't let Luke open all his presents in front of her on Christmas morning.'

I suppose this was the sort of inconsistency that the psychologist thought might be the problem, but I had to follow my maternal instincts a little, even now, when they seemed to be letting us down in every direction.

The next day we put it all behind us and enjoyed a

family Christmas as if the previous evening had never happened. I hoped that we could start the new year with a clean slate.

I should have known better than to indulge in such hopeless dreams.

24

Blades

After a few months of bureaucratic wrangling behind closed doors, the school and the LEA announced that they had managed to find enough money to hire someone to be with Sarah for half the school day. So she was allowed in for the mornings, but had to go home at lunchtime rather than be unsupervised during the afternoons. It was a start, although it added even more to the stigma she was already carrying as a child who was different from all the others.

Sarah tried to act as normally as she could, but it was all deeply upsetting for her. She had always been well liked and popular, part of the crowd. Now she was only permitted in school for the morning, before being marched through the deserted playground and out of the premises, because she couldn't be trusted alone. She was the girl people pointed at and whispered about, the one who had to spend every afternoon at home in case she damaged or stole or hurt something or someone. Her small shoulders seemed hunched under the burden of being ostracised and humiliated, but she rarely spoke about it. Instead, she carried on as best she could, treating this abnormal situation as part of her everyday life.

It made me want to weep to see her strange courage even while I longed to know why all this was happening to her, when it seemed that she had the power to stop it if she wanted to.

Then eventually, after six disruptive months, they found enough in the budget to hire someone for the full day. They decided they needed to hire three different people to do the job effectively, because they were afraid that if they had one full-time person, Sarah would work out what the woman's insecurities were and would manipulate her.

It was as if they believed she was some sort of evil genius. It was a reflection of my own worst fears. I had always thought Sarah was a bright girl, but I still found it incredible that she was able to work out such devious and cunning plans, and execute them with such skill that no one ever caught her or managed to work out how she could have done them. If I thought about it, I could see why they were starting to treat her as if she had superhuman powers, a sort of childish version of Hannibal Lecter.

There couldn't, they told me, be a single moment when she was left alone. She had to be followed in the playground and even to the toilet (so she stopped going to the toilet at all at school, to avoid the embarrassment of having someone observing her), and she had to have someone with her all the time in the classroom. I could understand why it was necessary, but it broke my heart that my little girl had to be treated like a convicted criminal or a potentially dangerous animal.

We also had to agree to play a part in keeping her under surveillance. Every morning, Mike and I had to search her clothes, her bag and her hands before she left the house in order to make sure she wasn't smuggling anything out that might be dangerous to the other children. It was so humiliating for her, but we had no choice.

However terrible it felt to have to subject her to so much suspicion, at least we had managed to get her back into the school, so her education wasn't going to fall any further behind. I also felt better knowing that there was no chance she could get at any of the other children now.

Then, to my horror and utter bewilderment, Tanya called me to say that some rusty Stanley knife blades had turned up in Amy's school bag.

I hardly knew what to say. My God, how could it be possible? Was Sarah really so endlessly bent on causing trouble? And was it really such an impossible task for all of us adults to keep control of one little child? I remembered how bemused the police had looked when they realised we couldn't control David all those years ago, but this was even more ludicrous.

Wearily, I trudged back into school to inform them of her latest trick.

'Ah,' the teacher said, as if that solved a mystery that had been puzzling her for some time. 'We found another of those on the library floor. We did wonder where it had come from.'

I had to believe that it was Sarah who had been responsible for both appearances of the dangerous blades. But how was she getting them past our search? She didn't deny it when I confronted her. As usual, she seemed resigned to being caught and punished.

Knowing now that there was a chance we could slice our fingers off in the process of searching her each morning, Mike and I started going about our guard duties with a great deal more care.

Tanya came round one afternoon with a worried look on her face. The moment I saw her, my heart sank and I dreaded to think what new disaster had befallen either her or Amy as a result of Sarah. The only thing I could be sure of was that whatever news she was carrying wasn't going to be good. I'd only just woken up and I was feeling tired and unwilling to spend hours going over some new problem, but I put the kettle on as she came into the kitchen anyway.

'When I came out of school with Amy this afternoon,' she said, before she had even sat down, 'I was looking for something in her pocket and found another Stanley blade.'

'Well, that can't be Sarah,' I said quickly, hardly daring to think about it, 'because you and Amy haven't even been anywhere near the house.'

Tanya looked hurt. 'Why are you being funny with me?' she demanded, as if I'd given her a slap. 'What are you accusing me for?'

'I'm not accusing you of anything. I just can't think how Sarah could have done it. She has someone following her around all day; how would she have been able to put a Stanley knife blade in Amy's pocket without them seeing?'

I realised it wasn't fair of me to take my frustration out on Tanya. She must have been just as disappointed as I was that Sarah was still up to her old tricks. She'd been very good about Sarah going back to the school and something like this was bound to worry her. Imagine, I thought to myself, if Amy had cut herself on one of these blades. How would I be feeling then?

I really didn't want to have to confront Sarah with this latest accusation, yet another in a seemingly endless stream, but I could see there was no alternative.

'Tanya found a blade in Amy's pocket,' I said. 'Do you know how it could have got there?'

'Yes,' she said, in the same resigned voice, her face an expressionless mask. 'I put it there.'

'How did you do that?' I asked, immediately feeling guilty for having snapped at Tanya.

'I went to give her a cuddle and slipped it into her pocket.'

'But how did you get the blade into school?' I asked. 'We search you and your bag every morning before we take you in. How did you get it past us?'

There was a pause while she thought for a moment,

and then she said matter-of-factly, 'It was in my shoe.'

I looked at her fingers and there were no signs of any nicks or cuts. How had she managed such a delicate feat without cutting herself? I was beginning to think she really must have supernatural powers.

I decided that this time I wouldn't go to the school and confess what had happened. They were already treating me like I was an incompetent mother and an attention-seeker. When I went to talk about the first blades they had more or less accused me and Mike of not searching Sarah properly before leaving the house in the morning and of being derelict in our duties by leaving blades where she could get them. They had even criticised me for allowing her to leave my side in the super- market while I was shopping. Apparently one of the dinner ladies had spotted her in an aisle on her own and reported back to the headmistress, who had rung me that evening.

'Why are you letting Sarah walk about the super- market on her own?' she demanded, sounding like she was talking to a five-year-old child. 'It would be very easy for her to steal a knife or something else sharp.'

Initially I was affronted to think I was being spied on and reported on. Then, when I'd cooled down a bit, I realised that perhaps they were right. But I still didn't like the idea that they were all talking about us behind our backs.

I knew Tanya had reported the latest blade incident so I decided I would wait to see if they informed me. I couldn't see that it would do any harm not to go in myself, as they were doing all they could to watch Sarah anyway. But the days passed and nobody from the school said a word to me. It was as if the incident had never happened.

I was still racking my brains to think of when Sarah could have planted her blade in Amy's pocket. I interrogated Tanya about whether Amy was wearing that coat the last time she came up to our house, but she couldn't remember, and I accused Mike of being too busy on his computer to watch Sarah carefully while I was asleep. It felt as if I had to stay with her myself every second of the day, since no one else was willing to do the job properly – though me being there didn't seem to make much difference. And why weren't the school letting me know what had happened? I had assumed they would have relished another opportunity to tell me off. They didn't know that Tanya had told me already. Had they given me up as a lost cause to responsible mothering?

I was furious at the whole world, and more than a little paranoid.

After a week had passed, I couldn't hold out any longer and I went back in to see the teacher.

'I believe you found a blade in Amy's pocket last week,' I said.

'Yes.' She seemed very guarded, as if frightened of giving something away.

'Well,' I went on, 'if you think it was my daughter who put it there, why haven't you talked to me about it?'

'We don't know for sure,' she said, as if she was the most reasonable person in the world, 'so we haven't said anything. We're dealing with it in our own way.'

'Hold on a minute. This is my daughter you're talking about. You have to at least let me know what's going on. I don't want anything hidden.'

She just looked at me and said nothing. What was she thinking? It was as if there was something else she didn't want to tell me. Knowing I wouldn't get any further that day, I gave up and went home.

One day after school Tanya picked Sarah up for me. When she dropped her at home, she told me she had found a slash in the back seat of her car, where Sarah had been sitting, and that there had been another blade on the floor just beneath it.

That evening, I took some of my frustrations out on Mike. 'How could you be so careless as to leave your

Stanley knife blades somewhere where Sarah can get hold of them?' I demanded.

'Are you sure these are Stanley blades?' he said, making me doubly irritated at the thought that he would try to distract me with technical details.

'Of course I'm bloody sure, I've seen them.'

'They actually have the word "Stanley" on them?'

'Yes, of course,' I snapped. 'Why?'

'They're not mine then.' He shrugged. 'I use the cheaper brand. She must have got them from some-where else.'

Now not only could I not understand how she had managed to get a blade into Amy's pocket without cut-ting herself, I couldn't imagine where she had got it from in the first place. Who in their right minds would allow Sarah near their tools, given her reputation? I couldn't think of a single possible candidate. She hadn't been anywhere except school and home for ages, cer-tainly not to anyone's house. It was extremely unlikely that the school would allow anyone to leave such dan-gerous things near any children, let alone Sarah. It was like she had a whole parallel life going on, where she organised all her crimes and then executed them before returning to the real world where the rest of us lived. But how did she manage to find the time when we were all watching her so carefully every minute of the day? I felt that my own sanity was slipping closer and closer to the edge as I tried to see some sense or logic in all of this madness.

25

Letters

Every time something terrible happened, Tanya would comfort me.

'It can't get any worse,' she would say.

But it always did.

'I wish you'd stop saying that!' I snapped after the latest incident with the blades.

'There's no need to take it out on me,' she said, looking like she might cry. 'I'm just trying to cheer you up.'

'I know.' I instantly felt guilty and ungrateful. 'I'm sorry, you've been such a true friend through all this.'

After the discovery of the blades, I had to admit that I thought she might finally be right. Surely there couldn't be anything worse that Sarah could do as long as we were watching her. She seemed to have run out of tablets, and she couldn't have unlimited access to blades. Opportunities for Sarah to do any damage were lessening as she became more and more isolated from the rest of the world. Most of her friends had stopped inviting her to their houses, and I had become nervous about even inviting her cousins to our house, in case something of theirs got damaged while they were with us.

I thought I had reached rock-bottom, but then the letters started to arrive.

My poor, damaged little daughter might have exhausted the opportunities open to her to do physical damage, but she had a whole new pool of psychological weapons ready and primed for action.

———————

She started by writing to Tanya, laboriously addressing the envelopes in her childish hand, although occasionally getting them upside down by mistake, and then putting them in the post when I wasn't looking, although I couldn't for the life of me work out when that was. She never bothered to put stamps on them, so Tanya had to pay the excess postage, which seemed a bit like adding insult to injury.

The first one contained a sheet of paper with some

poo smeared on it and a Diocalm tablet enclosed. That was disturbing enough, but it got worse. Far worse.

The next letter said,

Tanya sex me

Tanya was terrified I would think she had been doing something bad with Sarah, especially as I knew all about her past. I didn't know why Sarah would write such a thing, but I was pretty sure she would have told me if anything had been going on that she was unhappy about. I trusted Tanya because she was always so open when talking to me about her past – more open than I was always comfortable with, if I was honest.

It didn't occur to me that anything implied by those three words could have been happening – I was just puzzled as to why Sarah would want us to think it had been. Maybe she hadn't thought Tanya would tell me about the letter, but if that was the case, why would she want to accuse Tanya of such a thing? She must have known Tanya would tell me so she must have wanted to drive some sort of wedge between us. Perhaps she was jealous of our friendship, as one of the experts had suggested right at the beginning. This new development led to hundreds of new questions, and none of the possible answers were pleasant.

One afternoon Tanya and I were shopping in the local supermarket while the girls played around together. Tanya said she just had to pop to the toilets and I carried on shopping while she was gone. When she came back, she had the look I dreaded on her face again, and she was holding a bit of paper in her hand.

'I found this in the toilet,' she said, 'all screwed up. Sarah must have been in there and left it.'

She passed it to me reluctantly and I read the words.

I hate mummy mummy is a bitch mummy sex me

It was Sarah's handwriting.

I called Sarah over and asked her if she'd written it and she immediately started to get upset and deny it.

'But it's in your handwriting,' I said, feeling a wave of despair sweeping over me.

I couldn't get any sense out of her. With a heavy heart, I told the school that Sarah was now sending unpleasant letters, but didn't tell them what was in them. The implications were too awful and I didn't want to think about them.

Then Tanya intercepted another in Sarah's room before she got a chance to post it. It was addressed to the headmistress, saying,

I hate daddy my daddy hurts me

I was horrified, knowing that she must be referring to the one and only time that Mike had hit her in a moment of anger and exasperation. I could just imagine what the repercussions would be if a letter like that had actually got to the headmistress. The chances were the children would be taken away from us within hours and the onus would be on us to prove that we were suitable parents if we wanted them back. Given everything that had happened over the previous eighteen months, that would not be an easy task.

I thought perhaps I should be a bit more proactive about searching her room myself and so, after Tanya had left, I went upstairs to have more of a root around, to see if I had the same luck as Tanya. Within a few minutes I'd found another note in one of her drawers. It read:

Dear mummy
    I'm up the club with my boyfriend and he is licking my minny

As always, I panicked, desperate for someone who could advise me. All I wanted to do was run up to the school, get Sarah out and hug her and protect her. I rang the family therapist, babbling on about what I had found and begging for some guidance.

'Just leave her to the end of school as normal,' she advised, 'and deal with it when you come home. Do you think she's been abused?'

'I don't know.' My mind was racing. 'I don't think so, but I don't know.'

I tried to do as she suggested. I picked Sarah up from school as normal, but I couldn't hold on till we got home. I suggested we sit down under a tree on the way to the car.

'Do you want to talk about these letters?' I asked very calmly. 'Do you want to tell me what they mean?'

First I gave her the one Tanya had found about hating Mike. The moment she read it, she burst into tears.

'Don't tell Daddy I wrote this,' she begged. 'I don't want to hurt his feelings. He'll be really upset.'

'But why did you write it? What do you mean when you say Daddy hurts you?'

'That time when he smacked me. I think that's why I wrote it. Can I buy him a bar of chocolate to make up for it?'

'Of course you can. But don't worry, Daddy won't be upset. He wouldn't hurt you for the world. He just lost his temper that one time, that's all. He really regretted it afterwards.'

'I know,' she said, wiping her eyes dry and blowing her nose on the tissue I was offering.

I felt a wave of relief. If that was the only incident that she could think of, then at least there was nothing new to worry about. We had a hug and then I showed her the other letter.

'And do you want to tell me what this is all about?'

This time she started giggling, taking me completely by surprise. There were no tears and no denials, just a coyness and a blush of embarrassment. It was a completely different reaction from what I was used to.

'That's what me and Lucy wrote,' she said, referring to another of her friends who had been to the house a while before.

'But Lucy's a year younger than you,' I said, newly horrified that there was another child involved, but relieved that at least she remembered writing it. 'How on earth do the two of you know about these things?'

I immediately blamed Mike for not always keeping an eye on what the children were watching on television when he was in charge. Yet another example of what lax parents we were.

'I saw it on the television in Tenerife,' she said. 'Remember?'

'What?' For a second I couldn't imagine what she

meant. Then the memory came flooding back; when we'd all been watching television in the apartment during our holiday, a satellite station had popped up by mistake on the screen when the children were surfing through the stations. It had only been on for fifteen seconds at the most before I managed to get rid of it, but there had been a scene of oral sex going on. I had completely forgotten about it, but obviously Sarah had not!

'Well, that is not appropriate,' I blustered, not wanting her to see just how relieved I was that for once we had a logical and relatively harmless explanation. In the normal run of things, I would have been horrified to think that my children remembered seeing even fifteen seconds of porn, but compared to the horrendous pictures that had been playing out in my imagination ever since finding the note, it was nothing.

'You shouldn't talk about things like that!' I scolded half-heartedly.

'Well, you should ring the hotel and complain, then, shouldn't you?' she said, reverting to being Miss Clever Clogs. 'You should tell them it shouldn't be on the telly.'

'Yes,' I laughed. 'Actually, you're completely right.'

I gave her a huge hug and I could see that she was quite surprised by how lightly she had got off. Perhaps she was beginning to think what an inconsistent parent I was as well!

'But you really mustn't talk about things like that,' I persisted, trying to be sensible, 'unless something has happened to you that you need to tell me about.'

'OK,' she said, and we went to the sweetshop to get some chocolate for Mike.

―――――――

A few days later another letter fell out of Amy's clothes after she and Sarah had been playing. It said,

I hate daddy daddy sex me Daddy is a cunt

'But she doesn't even know that word,' I protested to Tanya when she showed me the note, 'let alone how to spell it correctly. Where would she have learned it? I never use it!'

Tanya looked a bit sheepish. 'She may have got it from Amy,' she said. 'David taught it to her the other day. I'm so sorry.'

When she said that, I did remember telling David off for using it in front of me once. Like a lot of women, it is the one word I just can't stand to hear, especially from the mouth of a child.

'Did you learn that word from Amy?' I asked Sarah later, and she nodded distractedly, apparently uninterested in listening to yet another lecture from her constantly angry mother. It seemed we had gone back to the denials and disinterest. The cheerful confession to the other letter had only been a temporary blip.

When I showed the latest note to Mike that evening, he said absolutely nothing. As far as he was concerned it wasn't even worthy of a comment, let alone a denial. Although I would have liked him to have shared my anxiety, I was relieved to see that he didn't show a flicker of guilt, even though I hadn't believed for a second that he would. I was absolutely sure that Mike would never do anything like that.

If the letters were indicating that Sarah was being abused, then it had to be someone outside the family. But I had never left my children with anyone apart from Tanya and, very occasionally, my parents. There could have been an incident in a playgroup somewhere, at some moment when I had thought she was being supervised and she wasn't. And there was a park at the end of the road that she sometimes used to walk up to with other children before she was put under twenty-four-hour surveillance.

'Has anybody ever tried to do anything to you?' I asked her one day. 'Or touched you down there in your minny?'

'No.' She wrinkled her nose up in disgust at the thought, shaking her head in despair at her mother's mucky mind.

'What would you do if they did?' I persisted.

'I don't know,' she replied, exasperated at my stupidity, 'because they haven't, have they?'

'If anyone ever does anything like that to you and tells you to keep it a secret because your mummy will hate you if you tell her, or won't believe you, that isn't true. You can always tell me anything and I won't be angry and I'll sort it out.'

'OK,' she said, obviously puzzled by my sudden vehemence about a subject that didn't seem to be bothering her at all. 'I'll tell you if anything happens. But nothing has. Can I go and play now?'

'Yes,' I sighed, 'of course.'

So much of the time she was just so normal, behaving exactly like every other little girl of her age. Why couldn't she be like that all the time? Why did she have to have this terrible black, secret side to her character?

I completely believed her when she said no one had interfered with her, but I couldn't help wondering if every mother of an abused child goes through the same process of disbelief followed by a gradual realisation that the unthinkable has actually happened. Do they all think that it is impossible for anyone they know to do such a thing? Do they all feel confident their child would tell them the moment anything went wrong? Was I kidding myself? My instincts told me that wasn't the problem, but then again I no longer completely trusted my instincts: all along, they had told me that Sarah would never do the sorts of things that she had been doing and they had to be wrong.

Something was going wrong inside my child and the possibility of abuse being the trigger had to be considered. I was sure this same thought was crossing the minds of the many experts I kept ringing up and begging for help. Tanya was the only person I could talk openly to about my worries, because I knew she would not be shocked, having been through so much of that sort of thing herself.

The letters were soon arriving at Tanya's house at the rate of one or two a week, but I couldn't understand how Sarah was getting the time to go to the postbox on such a regular basis, let alone write them. But it was definitely her writing, so there was no point denying that she was sending them, and they were always in the sort of cheap brown envelopes that Mike used for his work, which she could easily help herself to from his desk. Whoever would have thought that we should have been hiding our envelopes along with all the other potentially lethal weapons? And why was she becoming so obsessed with sex? Was this her way of telling us something terrible had happened to her — or was it something else entirely?

The questions kept on multiplying, but there were still absolutely no answers.

I was relieved that it was Tanya who was receiving the letters, rather than someone else, but it was still embarrassing. To make things worse, Tanya would tell me on the way to school, in front of Sarah, each time another one had arrived. As a result, Sarah would make herself ill with worry all day, knowing she was going to be in trouble in the evening, apparently unable to remember what she had written or why.

'Maybe you should just refuse to pay the postage,' I suggested to Tanya one morning, when she said another one had turned up. 'Then the postman won't deliver them and you won't have to read any more of them.'

But she convinced me it was better we knew what Sarah was writing, just in case it gave us a clue as to what was going on in her mind.

On the other hand, I suggested, if Sarah thought no one was reading them, perhaps she would stop sending them. But Tanya didn't seem to agree with that either.

Other letters were turning up in Amy's pockets anyway, saying,

I hate Amy and Amy is a bitch

So even if Tanya had stopped taking them off the postman, Sarah would have found a way to get them through to her somehow. Amy found it very upsetting to think that her best friend was writing such terrible things about her, and I knew exactly how she felt.

A little bit later, Tanya received another envelope from Sarah, containing a ten-pound note, with

I hate mummy mummy sex me

written on it in pen and some nasty-looking brown stains.

'I think that's poo again,' Tanya said, as she showed me.

It just seemed like there was never going to be an end to this. I decided to be practical. I scribbled over the words so they were illegible and washed the note, just in case the stains were poo. The way things were going, I couldn't afford to throw any money away, even when it doubled as a poison-pen letter.

One evening, after he had bumped into Tanya coming out of Sarah's room with yet another letter, Luke was speaking his thoughts aloud as he and I sat peacefully together in front of the television.

'It's funny, isn't it?' he said pensively.

'What's funny, darling?' I asked, only half listening.

'That it's always Tanya who finds these letters.'

'She's been a good friend to us,' I said.

'No one ever listens to kids,' he muttered.

'No,' I said, after a moment's thought. 'You're right, no one does ever listen to kids. It's not fair, is it?'

Sometimes Luke could be a very wise ten-year-old, but, like all the other grown-ups he was complaining about, I wasn't really listening to what he was saying. I was too distracted with my own thoughts and worries.

26

The Police Arrive

Then things got even worse and Sarah's friend Lauren received one of her hateful letters.

I hate you and I am going to get you at school from Sarah

Again, it was Sarah's untidy writing, with some of the letters characteristically formed backwards, although how she had managed to find out and spell Lauren's address so perfectly I wasn't sure. The street name was long and would have challenged anyone. Again, the letter had been posted without a stamp and Lauren's mum, Karen, had to go to the post office to collect it, unaware of what she was about to read.

Not surprisingly, the moment Lauren opened the letter and showed it to her, Karen was straight on the phone to me. She'd been a supportive friend up until then, even when the tablets had turned up in her daughter's pockets, but this was a direct threat to Lauren and she went mad. I would have done just the same if I had been in her shoes. Most mothers' first instincts are always to come to the defence of their own children.

I went round to see them, trying as usual to work out how Sarah had managed to get another letter in the post without me noticing. As I turned into the end of their street, I wondered if she had noticed its name on the sign when we were driving past. We had been there often enough, I supposed, for it to imprint on her memory. Still, even if she had been plotting away and took a note of it, it was still a very long word for a child to be able to spell correctly. It made me shiver to think what must be going on in her mind all the time, as she constantly schemed and planned her next move without me having the slightest idea what was going on. It was hard to understand how she could have done something like this without remembering it. It just didn't make sense.

'Did you ever give Sarah your address?' I asked Lauren,

once I'd seen the evidence and I was trying to show Karen how seriously I was taking the situation.

'No.' Lauren shook her head, as if puzzled why I would think she might have. Kids just know where their friends' houses are; they don't bother with addresses most of the time, especially if their parents drive them around a lot.

Karen was still not happy. I could tell she wasn't willing to let me handle things and I could understand that, as I hadn't done a very good job so far.

'I'm going to ring the police this time,' she threatened. 'I should have done it before.'

'OK,' I agreed, 'that's fine. I think you probably should.'

I had been suggesting to Tanya that she call the police about the letters for some time, but she never wanted to involve them, telling me she was frightened what they would turn up about her past, and saying she was sure we could all sort it out for Sarah. I had a lot of respect for the police and I thought they might be able to shed some new light on the problem that was mystifying us all. They might be able to get to the bottom of what it was that was troubling Sarah and they might have some suggestions on how we should be dealing with her. Once she was sending malicious letters, it was hard to see how they couldn't be brought in to the situation.

'Would you ring up social services for me as well if I

find you the number?' I asked Karen. 'All the people I've seen so far at the school, and the family therapist, have rung them, explaining that I'm at the end of my tether and begging them to help me, but they just don't take any notice. I'm supposed to have an allocated worker, but I never hear from him. If they think another child is in danger, they might react.'

I'd given up ringing social services myself because I got a different person each time and had to start the whole story from the beginning, which seemed completely pointless. One of them even asked me if I wanted them to take Sarah into care.

'Of course I don't,' I snapped, incredulous that they would even think that.

'What do you expect us to do then?' they wanted to know.

I had hoped they were going to be the ones suggesting what I should do, rather than the other way round. If someone else rang them with a complaint, perhaps they would start to take my situation a bit more seriously.

Following Karen's call to the police station, a young policeman went to see her and spent some time listening to the whole story. In the course of chatting to him, Karen mentioned how Tanya had received a lot of the same sort of letters.

'I know Lyndsey's her best friend,' Karen said, 'but if

my best friend's daughter was sending me those sorts of letters, I would be wanting to tell somebody.'

The policeman took it all seriously, noting down everything Karen was telling him, which encouraged her to spill out all the things she knew or had heard on the local grapevine. When it was all strung together like that, it must have sounded like quite a dramatic tale of a little girl unravelling, beginning with damaging and muti-lating her home and family's possessions, leading to stealing money, medication and dangerous blades, and finally to sending threatening letters to her friends. Unlike social services, who never seemed to be able to decide which calls they would or wouldn't follow up, the young policeman took what Karen had told him and decided to make a few further inquiries.

Tanya knew nothing about Karen's call and was obvi-ously shocked to find the policeman on her doorstep later that day. The moment he had asked his questions and gone, she rang me sounding flustered, warning me that he was on his way to me next.

I felt bad for Tanya – I knew that the last thing she wanted was the police involved. She was terrified of having her past exposed and dragged out into the public domain with whatever consequences that followed. I hoped that wasn't going to happen because of me. As

I waited for the knock on the door, I began to feel nervous. It was dawning on me that this policeman now knew Sarah was accusing me, her father and my best friend of sexually abusing her, and that she was showing highly disturbed patterns of behaviour. What if the police took the poison-pen notes at face value and decided the children needed to be protected from their parents? I could see at once that it might be a logical step for them to think they should make sure Luke and Sarah were somewhere safe while they completed their investigations. The idea made my blood run cold – I didn't know how I'd cope if my children were taken away from me. It was the worst thing any mother could imagine.

I was determined not to have to find out.

By the time the policeman arrived on my doorstep, I was feeling deeply defensive and ready for a fight to protect my babies. I went straight on the offensive.

'If you want to know anything about me, you come and ask me to my face,' I stormed.

'No, Mrs Harris,' he said very politely, deflating my anger and making me realise I was talking nonsense, 'that is not how we work.'

I took a deep breath and invited him in, sitting him down with a cup of tea. I was always ridiculously grateful to anyone who was willing to give up their time to listen to my worries and woes. As he drank his tea, I let all my troubles pour out again. He was a very nice young man and listened to my story carefully, taking notes as he went. By the time he left I felt that he had given me a fair hearing and he didn't seem to have jumped to any conclusions or judged me badly in any way. I would have to wait and see what the outcome was but once again, I allowed myself a tiny glimmer of hope that perhaps this nightmare was close to being over.

There was still no response to Karen's call to social services.

The next morning Karen was making a big fuss up at the school, saying she didn't want Sarah at the school any longer and that she was worried about Lauren's safety, which was fair enough. There wasn't much I could say, so I just kept quiet and hoped for the best. I didn't know what I would do if Sarah actually carried out her threat and hurt Lauren, although I was fairly sure she wouldn't. She hadn't actually hurt anyone physically at any stage and there seemed little danger that she would start now, but who knew what she was secretly planning?

'There's nothing we can do about it,' was the head-mistress's official line to Karen, 'because the incident happened outside the school.'

'In that case I'm taking Lauren out of school,' Karen told them. 'I'm not leaving her here and just waiting until that child does something to her.'

I had left Sarah with a heavy heart that morning, aware that she looked as bewildered and sad as I felt, and I had gone home, completely unable to think what I should do next. I felt numb as I waited for the consequences I was sure were coming. Half an hour later, I received a call from the school asking me to come and pick Sarah up because she had been excluded until further notice.

'I thought you couldn't do anything about it because the incident didn't happen on school property,' I said, knowing even as I spoke that it was pointless to struggle against the inevitable any more. I had to face it, I couldn't control my daughter and I had no idea what was wrong with her. I was a failure as a parent and I couldn't expect other parents and teachers to be able to cover for my failings for ever.

They had obviously decided they couldn't keep Sarah at the school if it meant other parents were going to take their children away, particularly as we weren't even living in their catchment area. They'd had enough of the whole thing and wanted rid of us. It was time for someone else to see what they could do with our difficult family. They told me they would be having a meeting with the educational psychologist at the end of the week and would let me know the outcome. This time I didn't even have the energy to insist that I came to the meeting. I wasn't sure that I could face listening to the whole thing again. They didn't mention to me that the meeting was going to involve the police and the social services, but I could tell there were things going on that I couldn't be included in. It was beginning to feel as though matters were being taken out of my hands, and the whole thing was taking on a life of its own with all of us helpless victims carried along with it.

My greatest fear looked closer than ever. What if they tried to take the children? I was terrified that I would hear a knock on the door and that our family life together would be over.

By the end of the week I had still heard nothing from the school or the police. We were existing in limbo. Now that we were out of the school, we were no one's responsibility and I could imagine they were all glad to be rid of us. I rang Tanya, wanting to have a big moan about the school and hoping for some sympathy, but for the first time in our fourteen-year friendship she just didn't seem interested.

'Oh well,' she grunted, 'I suppose you'll hear something next week.'

'Well,' I huffed, 'if it's too much trouble to talk to me . . .' and I hung up. Why was everyone acting so strangely? It was as if they all knew what was going on and I didn't. My child's future was being decided by a group of people who didn't think I should have a say, and even my best friend was fed up with hearing about my problems. I didn't see how things could get much worse. My hopes were fading again, and fast.

A couple of nights before that phone call, Tanya had come up to the house.

'Have you still got all that material you got me to write about my childhood?' she asked.

'Yes,' I said, wondering why she had suddenly thought about that.

When she had first started pouring out the torrent of memories of her abuse, I hadn't really known what to say to her so I had suggested that it might help her if she wrote it all down. She had liked the idea and had given me the resulting pages, which we had discussed in great detail for many weeks. Now she suddenly wanted the pages back. It was almost as if she was worried I might show them to someone else, although I had never given her any cause to doubt my loyalty or discretion. I was still keeping meticulously to my promise and had never breathed a word to anyone of her problems.

'Can I have them?' Tanya asked.

'Sure,' I said, more than happy to hand them over. They had not made for pleasant reading and I didn't feel in the mood even to think about her problems when I was so weighed down with my own. She took the pages from me and went out into the garden, where she set fire to them, watching until every last page had blackened and curled and flaked away to nothing. It was almost as if she was destroying the evidence of her past. I wondered if she was worried I might show them to the police and they would use them in some sort of prosecution of her father and Frank and the others who had treated her so badly. As far as I knew, there was no other evidence. If she refused to talk about it to anyone else, all her secrets would remain locked safely away.

'I've had enough of all this going on in my head,' she said, as if that was all the explanation I needed.

Now, to my astonishment, she was hardly ever taking my calls.

'What on earth is the matter, Tanya?' I would ask when I did manage to get through to her. 'Why don't you want to talk to me?'

It was hard to get any sense out of her. She just mut-

tered the familiar line about how I would hate her when
I found out the truth about what she had done.

'Oh, Tanya, you know that I would never hate you,'
I said, irritated that she was trying to turn the attention
back to herself when I felt I was the one who really
needed support, being on the verge of losing my children. 'Have I ever hated you for any of the other things
you've told me?'

I was nervous that if I gave her any encouragement at
all I was going to have to hear about yet more dreadful
sexual perversions that had happened to her down the
years, when my head was so full of my own worries. I
knew it was my duty as a friend to listen if she wanted to
talk, but I had to admit that it was very wearing, not to
say distressing. But I was beginning to feel numb to her
troubles after the relentless succession of stories, each more
grim than the last. It was harder and harder to waken my
sympathy, especially now I was so desperate for understanding myself. As she now seemed reluctant to talk to
me if she didn't have to, I took the opportunity to draw
back a bit and spend some time on my own or with Sarah,
just waiting to see what was going to happen next.

Unknown to me, the latest meeting in the school which
took place without us was attended by a policewoman
from the Child Protection Squad called WDC Holly

Townsend. The school informed her that they believed they had worked out what was going on with Sarah. They had realised, they told her, that Sarah wasn't the one who was doing all the things she was accused of. It was obvious who the culprit was. Her mother was the one responsible and she was putting the blame on her daughter. It was a classic situation of Munchausen's syndrome by proxy. According to them, I was making Sarah ill on purpose, just to draw attention to myself through her. I was the one doing all the damage, sending the letters, leaving the pills and the blades around. All along, it had been me, her mother, clamouring for everyone to pay attention to me and heedless of the consequences for my poor innocent child.

It's just as well I had no idea they were saying that, because I would have gone completely mad. And that would have convinced them that they were right.

Looking back now, I can understand what led them to that conclusion, and why they told the police that the children needed to be taken away to a place of safety. Because I had been so honest with them, going in and telling them everything that happened as it occurred, and because no one could find anything wrong with Sarah mentally, and because no one ever actually saw her doing the things she was being accused of, they had finally reached the conclusion that she wasn't guilty. Of course, I'd been saying that right from the beginning, more or less begging them all to agree with me that it just didn't make sense. Eventually I had been fighting a losing battle and had to admit defeat. Puzzled by how a small child could think up so many devious schemes and always get away without being caught, they went back to basics and came to the obvious answer: she hadn't. So who was the next most likely culprit? Me, of course. The one who seemed to be doing all the talking and demanding all the attention.

'No wonder she's always taking her children up the hospital,' one of the mothers said to another when she heard this latest theory. And it was true, I had always been panicking whenever Luke or Sarah got one of their nervous stomach aches, terrified that I was missing the vital signs of appendicitis or something. I never had any faith in my own parenting abilities; I always wanted to get an expert to check out anything I was doing to re-assure me I wasn't doing more harm than good.

I remember one typical incident, when Sarah didn't want to go to school and told me she had damaged her ankle, so I was off up the hospital with her again. Tanya came with us and had carried Sarah all the way up the hill, because I refused to.

'I wouldn't carry her,' I said, sensing that Sarah was taking liberties. 'Make her walk.'

'No, it's all right,' Tanya said, with the air of saintly resignation she often adopted, 'I'll do it. Maybe I'll lose some weight.'

By the time the doctor came out to see her, Sarah had forgotten that she was supposed to be in pain and was trotting around the room, poking her nose into everything. She even had the nerve to expect Tanya to carry her back down the hill again afterwards!

When I later found out that the school believed that I had Munchausen's by proxy, I understood why they had stopped responding to my calls and why they looked so irritated whenever I went in. I dare say I was a pretty good pain in the neck. It also made sense that they were so eager to pounce on this explanation, since it all seemed to fit together so neatly. During the months that I believed Sarah was the one behaving oddly, I was forever looking things up on the Internet in my desperation to try to find a solution, and then rushing around telling everyone about every new discovery I made, grasping at any straw that came my way. When I came across a syndrome called 'opposition defiance disorder', for instance, I became convinced that Sarah must be suffering from it. I photocopied the web pages and sent copies to the psychiatrist, the school and the family therapist, whom we were still seeing every week. The therapist was the only one who took any notice of me.

WDC Holly Townsend was advised of my suspected condition at the meeting and it was suggested by the school that she should take Luke and Sarah into care as soon as possible, to get them away from their dangerous mother.

I had no idea that was what she had been told. Nor did I know that she had informed them she would like to make a few inquiries for herself before making that decision. Luckily for me, she was not the sort of woman who was going to let anyone railroad her into doing anything before she was ready.

'This has been going on for eighteen months now,' she said to them. 'The children don't seem to have come to any physical harm. A few more days won't make any difference. It may be that it is indeed the mother doing all these things, or the father, but it is also possible it is someone else. I want to learn a little bit about the family dynamics before I start removing the children from their home.'

Thank God she was such a sensible woman. I can only imagine the harm it would have done our family if someone else had been allocated our case and they had allowed themselves to be influenced by everyone else's opinion and had taken the children away. Because of Holly's refusal to panic, I was given a few more days leeway, although I still had no idea how close the danger was.

27

The Confession

Even though I didn't know that we were within days of the children being taken away, I did realise that if Sarah went on behaving the same way, it wouldn't be long before someone else's mother put in a complaint and the police would be forced to act. Time was obviously running out for the whole family. I couldn't think of anything else to do but what I had been for the last eighteen months.

However hard I racked my poor, tired brain, I could find no option other than to keep on going with our lives. That weekend I went into town with my shift manager, who is one of my best friends, to distract myself with a bit of shopping. It gave me a chance to clear my head and think for a moment. I realised that Tanya and I had not really been in touch for a while, and that I hadn't been giving her as much of my attention as I should have over the previous couple of weeks. When we had spoken, she had sounded very low and seemed to act strangely, not wanting to talk much.

'I'll put it right,' I decided. 'I'll ring her.'

Over the last year, very slowly, the stories of Tanya's past, and what was happening to her in her relationship with Frank, had become worse and more lurid. Sometimes I couldn't understand how so many appalling things could happen to one person, or how she managed to carry on with her normal everyday life.

I dreaded being told another story of violence and suffering, but I couldn't help worrying about how she was. I'd been doing it for too long to be able to break the habit just like that, and I was always particularly concerned about her when she was in a funny mood, knowing that she was probably being haunted by bad memories. She always appreciated my concern in the long run, saying she wished her mother or her sister were more like me and had showed a greater interest in her problems when she was younger. Taking a deep breath, I dialled her number.

When Tanya answered the phone, she was completely

and instantly hysterical, as if my call had come at a moment when she was already in the middle of some sort of noisy crisis.

'What's the matter?' I wanted to know, dreading to think how long it would take me to coax the story out of her when she was in a state like this, wondering if Frank had been round and there had been some sort of confrontation with Andrew.

'You'll find out everything,' she wailed, 'and you'll hate me for ever.'

'I'll never hate you,' I assured her, as I always did, but nothing I said would calm her down and I couldn't make head nor tail of what she was ranting on about.

'Is Andrew there?' I asked eventually, worried that she might be in the house on her own or, worse still, with Frank.

'Yeah, yeah, yeah!' she screamed, and I wondered if she had finally told him about all the abuse and the rapes and he had reacted badly. How would anyone cope, finding out the immense secrets his wife had kept from him for so many years? How would he deal with ongoing relationships and the dreadful violence Tanya had suffered without breathing a word? I could well imagine his initial reaction might be fury.

'Can I talk to him, please?' I said, hoping that he would

be able to shed some light on what was going on.

There was a long pause and then Andrew came on the line in his usual stuttering, hesitant way, unable to say whatever it was that needed saying.

'Just spit it out,' I said, feeling worried, but also tired and fed up with all the drama. 'What's going on?'

'Could you pop in on your way back from town?' he asked eventually.

I could tell he wanted to talk to me on his own for some reason. He had never wanted to talk to me alone ever. I must have guessed right, and he had found out about Frank and needed to speak to someone about it. I didn't know what I could say to help, but the least I could do was listen and be supportive. He might even be angry with me for not confiding in him.

As I drew up outside the house a little while later, I beeped the horn to let him know I was there. After a few moments he came out of the front door and climbed into the car with me.

'Can you take me back to your house?' he asked. 'I want to speak to you and Mike together.'

Perhaps this wasn't about Frank after all.

'Mike isn't there, he's gone out with Sarah. What's going on?' I demanded. 'I'm worried, I'm tired and now I'm scared. Just spit it out, Andrew, for God's sake.'

'Can you drive round the corner please?' he said, his hands tapping nervously on his knees, his eyes fixed on the house as if he expected Tanya to burst out at any moment and catch us.

Muttering to myself, I did as he asked, feeling increasingly annoyed by his dithering about.

Once we were out of sight of the house, I drew the car to a stop.

'What is all this, Andrew?' I said, exasperated. 'What's so important that we have to do all this cloak-and-dagger stuff?'

He didn't say anything but stared out of the window and then down at his lap where his hands were twisting nervously.

'Come on, then,' I snapped. 'What have you got to tell me?'

Andrew was never the quickest off the mark when it came to speaking but I was determined to get whatever it was out of him.

He opened his mouth and closed it again. I noticed suddenly that he was dead pale and that his hands were shaking.

'I'm worried now, Andrew. Is something wrong?'

He looked like he was in pain as he finally whispered, 'I'm really sorry.'

'Sorry? Sorry for what?' A sense of horrible unease was growing in me.

'All the trouble . . .' His voice was trembling, I noticed, and he couldn't meet my eyes. 'All the trouble you've been having with Sarah for the last eighteen months . . .'

'What about it?' I tried to nudge him on to finish his sentence, desperate to hear what he had to say. Something nervous fluttered in my stomach. 'What about Sarah?'

'It was all Tanya,' he said, his voice so quiet I wasn't sure I'd heard him right.

There was a stunned silence, while I tried to process what he'd just said. At last I managed to say, 'What do you mean, "It was all Tanya"?'

Andrew looked completely agonised. 'Everything you think Sarah did over the last year or more – she didn't do any of it. Tanya was responsible for all of it. She wrote all the letters, and planted the tablets and the blades and did all the cutting. And she stole the Christmas Club money.'

I was speechless. I literally couldn't say a word, as the realisation began to sink in. What had he said? That *Tanya*, my best friend, my support, my help, had done all this to me, and to my little girl? It was surely impossible! No, I wouldn't believe it.

'No, no,' I stuttered. 'You must have got it wrong!'

But at the same time, the pieces all fell into place so neatly that it was obvious that there was no one else who could have been to blame. He was right, I knew that completely, without a shadow of doubt. Sarah had never done any of the things I accused her of and I could suddenly see that it was impossible that she could have. Only Tanya could have done it. All the things that were too difficult for a child of seven − like slicing through a Hoover wire, hiding blades in her pockets without cutting herself, posting letters when she was being watched at every waking minute − had been done by an adult. It was clear now. What was most amazing was that it had never occurred to any of us that the only possible suspect was Tanya.

As it dawned on me that Andrew was telling the truth, a great fury, full of hurt and betrayal, boiled up inside me. I started shouting and screaming, as poor Andrew cowered next to me.

'How could she?' I yelled, pounding the steering wheel. 'How could she do this to me? To Sarah? What have we ever done to her? How could a child deserve this? It's the wickedest thing I've ever heard. For God's sake, Andrew, tell me why!'

While I raged at Tanya and her awful, treacherous

behaviour, I was desperately angry with myself. How could I have been so stupid for so long? Of course it all made sense. Who was the one person who had access to our house and to Sarah? Who had a key to our front door and could wander freely around the house whenever she felt like it? Who was the one I went to with every worry? Who was the person I had trusted so completely, because I had known her by then for fourteen years, that it had never entered my head to suspect her?

I could see exactly how it had worked now: I would tell her the story about Sarah wanting a bra and so she would know that Sarah would fall under suspicion when my bra was cut a few days later. She would know about Mike smacking Sarah that time. She knew when I would say that I thought things were improving and that would be her signal to do something else. She knew the things that were most precious to us all and what would most hurt us. She knew absolutely everything, down to the last detail, and she had used it all in her ceaseless campaign of sabotage.

It was like a light had switched on in my head and I couldn't believe that I hadn't worked it out for myself months before. Even when Luke had pointed out that it was only ever Tanya who found Sarah's nasty letters, the penny still hadn't dropped with me.

That was what she meant all those times she told me I would hate her when I found out what she was really like. Well, she was right. I couldn't believe what she had done to me or how she could watch as I nearly lost my mind and my children through her actions.

Why? That was what I couldn't understand. Why would she do this to me? Why would anyone want to inflict such damage on people who had only ever been her friends, however badly damaged they might have been in their own childhood? I wanted an answer. I *needed* an answer.

'We're going back to your house,' I snapped, once I had calmed down enough to speak coherently. 'Now!'

Andrew didn't protest, just sat looking miserable and mumbling pathetic apologies. Even then, I didn't want to take it out on him or his children. I knew they were as much her victims as we had been, but I wasn't sufficiently in control to be able to make him feel any better at that moment.

We drove back round the block and pulled up in front of the house.

'When did she tell you this?' I asked, trying to piece together exactly what the sequence of events had been.

'A few days ago,' he muttered, avoiding my eyes.

'A few days!' I couldn't believe my ears. 'How come it

took you this long to tell me? They're probably thinking of taking my children away, Andrew! Didn't you think you should do something?'

'I didn't believe her,' he said. 'She makes things up sometimes and I thought this was one of her imaginary stories. I thought it was some sick fantasy.'

I could certainly believe that. 'How did she manage to eventually convince you, then?' I demanded.

'When I didn't believe her, she confessed to David.'

'She dragged her own son into this?' I couldn't believe it.

'Yes,' he nodded. 'He believed her and he convinced me.'

'Go and get Amy and David out of the house because I'm going in to see her,' I told him and he went off obediently. He was a man who was used to doing as he was told.

Once the others had been cleared out, I went in, not sure what I was going to say. Her mum was there, but she avoided my gaze and neither of us could think of anything to say to each other. I climbed the stairs, calling out Tanya's name, and pushed open the bedroom door. She was lying on the bed with a pillow over her head, like a little child trying to escape a telling-off. I yanked the pillow away and hurled it across the room.

'What's going on?' I screamed. 'All these years I've put you before my family and you've destroyed Sarah's life! She's an innocent child who loves you and you've deliberately made her life a misery! What the hell have you been doing?'

She was snivelling and crying but didn't seem to have anything to say for herself.

'I don't know,' was all she mumbled. 'I don't know why.'

'All those times you stood by while I screamed and shouted at her and doled out punishments, and you just watched and smirked. You even used to encourage me to tell her off. Why would you do that? What has she ever done to you?'

I wasn't getting any sensible responses, just self-pitying whines as she moaned that it wasn't her fault. She wasn't even worth listening to, and I couldn't bear to look at her another second. I stormed back downstairs, where her mother was in the kitchen. I was still roaring with anger and looking for someone else to take it out on. The poor woman looked like she just wanted to run away, but she stood her ground a lot more bravely than her daughter.

'I'm not surprised she's screwed up if half the things she's told me about her childhood are true,' I spat.

She looked at me sadly. 'If she's been telling you her father abused her . . .'

I was taken aback. I'd always been meticulously discreet about Tanya's past, never telling anyone the things she had told me over the years in confidence. It was a shock to hear her mother admitting it openly. I didn't say anything; my tirade had been stopped dead in its tracks.

'She has, I can tell. The same old story. She's been telling people that ever since she was sixteen.' Tanya's mum sounded more exhausted than hurt. 'It's not true, of course.'

I was so confused now I had no idea if she was just repeating something Tanya had told her, or whether I was actually hearing the truth. I didn't have time to even try to work it out at that moment. There was too much to take in. Even so, I felt so sorry for her: it must be a terrible dilemma when your children do something you're ashamed of. You would still love them, I'm sure, and part of you would want to defend them and find excuses, protecting them from the consequences of whatever they have done, while another part would just want to hide away from the world in shame. God knows what the parents of serial killers and other monsters feel like. I didn't think this was the time to enlighten her on how Tanya used to tell me that her mother had watched while her father abused her. At that moment I couldn't find an ounce of pity in my soul for any of the ordeals that Tanya had been through. Nothing that had happened to her could ever excuse what she had done to Sarah and the rest of my family.

I didn't want to waste any more time even thinking about Tanya and her twisted past. As the events of the last few minutes sank in, the only thing I wanted to do was find Sarah to hug her as tightly as I could and tell her that all her problems were over. I had to beg her forgiveness for everything I had put her through – for what we had all put her through.

As I left the house, I realised that Tanya hadn't even said she was sorry.

All the way home my brain was racing at a hundred miles an hour, trying to put everything together. How could I have been so blind and so stupid for so long? My only comfort was that the victims of con artists always feel the same, devastated by their own gullibility and willingness to trust others. Now that I had the missing piece, the whole thing made sense.

It all began months and months ago, when the mysterious lighters were turning up in Luke's room. He had been Tanya's first victim, and she had begun by framing him as a little arsonist. But then she must have realised that Sarah would be an easier target: she had more access to her because of the girls' friendship. Luke had probably been spared simply because he wasn't as close to David as Sarah was to Amy. And perhaps we would have been more likely to believe Luke, as he was older and more capable of explaining himself.

As I drove, I began to cry, and soon the tears were streaming down my face. What had my darling little girl been through? I thought of how dignified Sarah had been when all the time she must have been thinking she was losing her mind. I felt so guilty as I remembered all the things I'd said to her over the months, all the punishments I had inflicted on her, all the embarrassment and humiliation that she had suffered at school.

We had all kept on at her so much she had actually ended up believing that she was doing all the terrible things. How frightened must she have been to think that she was capable of such acts and not even able to remember doing them? How noble she had been each time she had confessed to something she hadn't done, assuming it must have been her evil other half. What other explanation could there be?

The relief that the nightmare was over and the mystery explained was mixed with this awful guilt and distress for what Sarah had been forced to endure.

When I got home, there was no one there. I waited impatiently for Mike to return with Sarah. I had rung him and told him what I had discovered but he hadn't wanted to say anything to her, preferring to leave that to me. Mike's never one for big emotional scenes, even happy ones. Every minute seemed like an age as I waited to break the news to her.

'Sarah!' I ran over to her the moment she walked through the door, startling her. 'I am so, so sorry. I've just found out that you haven't been doing any of the things you've been accused of. It was someone else. You didn't do any of it. I know now that you were telling the truth all the time.'

To my surprise, she didn't even ask who the real culprit was. She just burst into tears of relief as we clung on to each other like we never wanted to let go.

'Oh, Mummy,' she said. 'I thought I was doing things in my sleep.'

For a few minutes it was like the whole house was charged with electricity, and then it passed, as though she was now happy to move on and continue her life as if it had never been interrupted. A little later that evening she went upstairs on her own with a pencil and paper. Having spent so many months being asked to talk about

333

feelings that she didn't have by doctors and teachers and therapists and me, she knew exactly how to analyse what she was feeling now. She knew the language she should use to get her emotions out on to paper; we had made her experienced in self-analysis at the age of seven.

'*To whoever did this this is how you've made me feel*', she wrote. '*angry scared worried sick*'. She drew little faces to illustrate each of the emotions.

Now that I had had the chance to absorb the truth, I found more questions bobbing to the surface. At last Sarah was able to give me answers.

'When the first money went missing,' I asked her later, 'right at the beginning, why did you say you'd taken it?'

'Because Luke was getting so upset,' she said, as if it were obvious. 'He gets really worried about that sort of thing. So I thought it would be better just to say I did it. But then you kept asking me what I had done with it and I didn't know what to say.'

'I'm so sorry, sweetheart. Mummy will never not believe you again.'

———

On the Monday after Tanya's confession, Mike and I went into school for a meeting with all the teachers who had been involved with Sarah's problems. I would be lying if

I said I wasn't looking forward to breaking the news to them. I had no idea at that time that they had reached the conclusion I was suffering from Munchausen's.

'Sarah is innocent. She didn't do any of it,' I declared, delighted that at last I had the answers to the mystery that had baffled us all. I explained that Tanya had confessed to everything. To my fury, I could see from their faces they didn't believe me. They must have thought that 'Munchausen woman' was just trying another ruse to get attention, and that I was stooping very low if I was willing to incriminate my faithful friend, a woman who had frequently been the target of my crimes.

Now they told me that they had involved the police in their meeting and that on the previous Friday they had advised that the children should be taken into care because they were in danger from me.

For a horrible moment, I wondered if I had dreamed the whole confession scene with Tanya. Maybe I was mad and deluded. Mike and I, faced with the prospect of losing our children even now, were stunned into silence.

As the teachers all sat there, staring at me patronisingly as if indulging me in my latest little fantasy, the school secretary knocked on the door and came in with an urgent message from a doctor who had been to see Tanya. He had received the same full confession she had given me. There was silence for a moment, and then the atmosphere suddenly changed. In their eyes, Sarah had already been cleared, so it was me they suddenly saw in a new light. I was vindicated. They could see now that I had been open and honest with them at every turn. Sarah was invited to go back to school that afternoon, just as if none of it had ever happened.

———————

I was full of anger, towards Tanya, and towards others who had been involved in our extraordinary drama. But mostly I was angry with myself for having been so gullible and stupid. I thought about how I used to fret over the children, convinced that I was an inadequate mother, and how hard I tried to do the right thing. Then I went and got the biggest thing in Sarah's life wrong. I had completely misjudged her and I didn't think I would ever be able to forgive myself.

'When you thought it was me,' Sarah said one day, 'I bet you wished I was never your daughter.'

'No,' I said, completely truthfully, 'I never wished that, ever. I might not have liked what I thought you were doing, but I never stopped loving you.'

'That's nice,' she said.

'I'm sorry I didn't believe you.'

I was struggling with my own emotions and worried that I wasn't going to be able to give her the support she would need as she came to terms with what had been done to her. Hoping that they might finally come round now that they knew I wasn't the mad mother of a demon child, I rang social services and asked if there was anyone who could chat to Sarah to make sure she was all right about everything, and that she wasn't holding anything back for fear of hurting my feelings. The rather arrogant-sounding man said they might send someone out, but they never did.

As time passed and Sarah got used to her new-found status as a heroine instead of despised outcast, she began to work out some useful angles for exploiting what she'd been through to her advantage. Thinking back over all the things she had missed or had had taken away from her, like the pocket money that had been stopped or the trips she had been forbidden to go on, she began to compile a mental list of all the things I now owed her. It seemed to me she was well on her way back to being a normal little girl. She admitted that she still felt angry with me, but I assured her that was completely understandable.

'It's right that you should feel angry towards me,' I said. 'I did misjudge you and I didn't have faith in you.

But you must remember that even when they had managed to convince me that it must be you, I still stuck
with you and searched as hard as I could for a way to
help you.'

28

The Aftermath

When I was finally visited by WDC Holly Townsend, I discovered she was a good-looking young woman with a firm, understanding manner. At first, I was a bit aggressive, complaining that no one had got back to me sooner. She wasted no time in letting me know that she was now in charge and things would move at the speed she wanted. There was something about her manner which made me think this was a woman who actually meant what she said, so I shut up and listened.

We talked for a long time and I explained my side of the story yet again. She gave no indication that she didn't have all the time in the world to listen to what

I had to say. I never need much encouragement to talk, and I was so busy babbling through the story that I now knew so well it was engraved on my heart that I didn't really notice how little she was saying. She was there to listen, and that was encouraging. She let me talk for ages, treating me as if I was a victim of the crime rather than the criminal, and wrote down my eighteen-page statement.

Even though I now knew what Tanya had done to Sarah and me, I still stayed loyal to her and said nothing about the things she had trusted me with. I told Holly there were reasons why Tanya was the way she was, but that I couldn't say what they were.

'I admire your loyalty,' was all she said.

I would get to know Holly very well in the coming months, and I gradually found out what an important role she had played in saving my children from being taken into care. Coming at the case fresh, not knowing any of the personalities involved, she had thought that it didn't feel right, and she had been determined to get to know more before jumping to any conclusions.

'It was just instinct,' she told me. 'Something told me that the letter to Lauren was not written by a child. The envelope was addressed upside down, which seemed deliberate. Most children are quite careful about that sort of thing. The most difficult words in the address were spelled perfectly. It just didn't seem right. But I wasn't going to jump straight to the conclusion it was you until I knew more about you.'

If only there were more people in the world with instincts like Holly's and the courage to follow them when everyone else was pointing in the opposite direction. But even though she had her doubts about me being the culprit, she didn't have any other idea who it might be until Tanya confessed.

If Tanya hadn't come clean, she would easily have been able to cover her tracks once she knew the police were looking into the case, and we would never have discovered the truth. If that had happened, Sarah might have spent the rest of her life believing that she had done those things in her sleep. Everyone else would have gone on thinking it was me who was behind the whole thing, and how could I ever have proved them wrong if nothing else happened after I was 'exposed'? If Holly had taken the children into care after the meeting with the school, I would have gone into overdrive to try to get them back, and with every phone call I made, every letter I wrote, every door I banged on and every official I berated, I would have confirmed the belief that I was nothing more than an attention-seeking madwoman.

If that had happened, if Tanya had never confessed, I might actually have ended up going mad for real.

Although Sarah didn't ask me who the guilty party was, which surprised me, Luke was desperate to know and kept pestering me to tell. It took me a little while to be able to tell them that it was Tanya, the woman they had seen as a second mother and a best friend. It seemed like a double betrayal, although Luke may already have worked it out. I couldn't get the pictures out of my head of all the times Tanya had stood by and watched as I shouted and screamed at Sarah, punishing her for crimes that Tanya knew full well she hadn't committed.

'I'm really sorry, Sarah,' I said. 'It was Tanya.'

'But she's my godmother,' she said, hardly able to take in this new piece of information. 'And I love her and she loves me.'

'I know,' I said, giving her a cuddle, 'but there is one thing you have to promise me, both of you. You mustn't be horrible to David and Amy about this. She's still their mum and none of it was their fault.'

Now that my confidence in my own judgement had been somewhat restored, I felt sure that I could trust both of them on this. They were good people, Luke and Sarah, and now no one would ever be able to convince me of anything different.

I felt so sorry for David and Amy. If Tanya had failed to apologise to me, David more than made up for it when I next saw him. The poor boy was devastated to discover what his mother had been doing and couldn't stop crying and apologising.

'It's not your fault,' I assured him. 'You must never think that.'

I was determined that he and Amy would not be made to suffer any more than they were bound to already. Tanya was still their mum, whatever she had done, and they were as much the injured parties as we were. She had used them in just the same callous way as she had used Sarah. She had ruined Amy's friendship with Sarah and no doubt caused her a great deal of hurt and worry. She purposefully wrecked all those birthday parties and other family events. I remembered the terrible way Christmas Eve had ended for everyone and how she had even suggested David might be implicated in some of the crimes. She had been willing to frame her son for her own vicious and pointless crimes.

———

As the days rolled by, the news spread through the grapevine and everyone found out the truth. Other missing pieces of the jigsaw were given to me by people who didn't even realise they held them. Because the school had become convinced that I was the culprit, other parents had stopped telling me about some of the things that happened, which they assumed I had been responsible for. A photo of Sarah had turned up in the toilets, with the eyes gouged out. Had they asked me about it, I would have been able to tell them that only Tanya had a copy of that particular picture and perhaps we might have worked out what was going on a little more quickly.

Andrew discovered that a packet of his Stanley knife blades had disappeared, with exactly the same number of blades in it as had been found in pockets and bags and around the school. As the true story spread around the area, a surprising number of people told me that they'd always thought Sarah was innocent. I couldn't help wondering why they hadn't had the decency to speak up for her at the time if that was the case. But then, I had been conned into going against my instincts too, so I couldn't really blame them. Others were more honest and admitted they too had been fooled.

'I'm so sorry,' the family therapist said when she found out. 'I should have worked it out.'

'How could you?' I said. 'You were only going on what I told you, and I hadn't worked it out.'

'But I should have asked you the one vital question,' she said.

'What was that?'

'Had anyone actually seen Sarah doing any of the things she was being accused of? If we had just concentrated on that, and maybe thought outside the box a bit, we might have realised that it had to be someone else.'

It's easy to be wise after the event, and it's easy to jump to conclusions simply because there isn't any other obvious explanation for something. The legal system understands all that, which is why it demands that there is evidence before someone is convicted of a crime, or that the jury is convinced 'beyond all reasonable doubt' of a defendant's guilt. There was always so much reasonable doubt that Sarah could have been the perpetrator of all those crimes, yet we all convicted her in our minds. How many times, I wondered, do adults assume that a child is guilty of something, just because we all know that children can be wilful and spiteful sometimes, and because we know that they make bad judgements and then try to cover their mistakes with lies? We know all those things and so we jump to conclusions. Luke was perfectly right when he said, 'No one ever listens to kids.' Not even their mothers, it seems.

The police were determined to charge Tanya with something that would be serious enough to get her a prison sentence, but because it was such an unusual case they had a lot of trouble working out which charges would best fit the crime. They didn't want it to be just a harassment charge, because they could see now that there was a great deal more to it than that. Holly was endlessly patient, and rang me regularly to let me know exactly what was going on. She was always honest and up front with me, even if she thought the news might upset me, which I found so refreshing after having so many people whispering behind my back for so long.

———————

The confession had happened in August, and it wasn't until the following March that the case finally came to court. During that time Tanya was still at home, living her normal life, except that she obviously didn't have anything to do with any of us. She didn't take Amy into the school buildings any more either, being keen to avoid the other parents, particularly me. But Sarah saw her driving around the area a few times. Andrew doesn't drive so she still had to do the school runs.

'I couldn't do anything, Mummy,' she told me that evening, 'because Amy was there, but I felt like sticking my fingers up at her.'

I was proud of her for managing to restrain herself for Amy's sake, but I didn't see why she had to see Tanya at all. Luke found it hard to see her too, telling me that she seemed to be smirking at him as she drove past. I could imagine exactly the expression he was referring to — I'd seen it a thousand times over the years — and so I asked Andrew if there was any way he could ask her to drop the children further down the road, which she did start doing from then on.

Whatever else Tanya had done, she had brought her children up well. They impressed me with their mature reactions and the way they leapt to defend Sarah when they could have gone the other way completely.

In particular, Amy was very sweet and brave. She actually made an announcement to all the children on their table at lunch.

'It wasn't Sarah who did all those things,' she told them. 'It was my mummy.'

Her honesty touched me deeply. I thought that showed a lot of courage and I felt so sorry for her because, for obvious reasons, Tanya missed Amy's leavers' concert, realising she wouldn't be welcome at any school events. Andrew was very good at filling the gap she had left in their children's lives, making sure he always went to everything, but seeing him on his own can only have reminded Amy of what had happened. It must have been terribly hard for her.

I would have been happy to help drive David and Amy around, knowing that Andrew couldn't drive, but Tanya wouldn't allow me to have anything to do with them. I thought it would be better for them if things stayed as normal as possible, and I had been a big part of their lives up to then. Tanya couldn't face it, though.

With her love of self-dramatisation, Tanya had told her children there was a possibility she might go to prison long before it was known what would happen to her, which was something else the poor kids had hanging over their heads for months.

'If Mummy goes to prison,' Amy said to me one day when she'd spotted me after school, 'will I still be able to come to Sarah's birthday party?'

'Of course, sweetheart,' I said, my heart going out to her. 'You're always welcome here, you know that.'

I was scrupulous to be fair to Tanya's poor children. I didn't want them to suffer and hated the idea that they would have to see their mother go to prison. But I had a deep need for vindication. I don't think it was a thirst for revenge that made me spend hours helping Holly build up a case against my former friend. It was, I think, a need to see justice done for my family. And I wanted answers. Why had Tanya done it? And why had she confessed? I was desperate to find out.

29

The Depth of the Deception

As I began to come to terms with the extent of Tanya's deception, my thoughts turned back to the stories she had told, stories of rapes and attacks and pregnancies and dead babies that had become more and more bizarre in recent months. If she had been capable of this sustained campaign against our family, she was certainly more than capable of making up these tales. There was a strong chance that nothing Tanya had ever told me was true. I began to realise that everything had been an invention designed to hold my attention.

This realisation shocked me profoundly, and it was hard to confront it, so I approached it slowly, taking my time, thinking back over everything she had said to me.

Once I began to accept the fact that Tanya had made me the victim of an incredible number of lies, I felt released from my promise to her to keep it all a deadly secret. First, although I found it deeply difficult and stumbled over my words, I confided in Holly. She listened patiently to every word when I finally managed to get them out, and never made any judgement about my stupidity and gullibility. On the contrary, she took a fantastic amount of time and effort to reassure me that none of it was my fault.

Then I was able to discuss with Andrew and with Tanya's parents some of the stories she had told me, and that I had entirely believed. Everything began to collapse under scrutiny. From the family abuse through her encounters with paedophiles and rapists, to Frank himself, who had frightened me so badly: it had all been a tissue of fabrication.

Andrew and I talked about how Tanya liked to pretend she was someone else when she was online.

'She used to spend hours talking to you under different names,' he reminded me. 'But you know about some of the names she used because you got cross with her.'

'Even though I knew she used to do that sometimes

to wind me up, I never guessed for a second that she was Frank,' I confessed. 'I feel so dumb. It's so obvious when I think back now. Every time he was online to me and I tried to ring, your phone would be engaged. But I had been hearing about Frank and how he beat her up in the past for so long . . . She was so convincing when she was being "him". One minute he would be telling me he hated Tanya, the next moment he would say he loved her. He used to tell me he hated me too, and wanted to make me suffer. Then he would tell me he fancied me from photos he'd seen and wanted to meet me.'

I could guess now that Tanya knew how terrified I was of Frank and she was safe in thinking I would never agree to meet him.

'She told me that she had made up that first story about being beaten up by an abusive boyfriend,' Andrew said. 'She told me that the boyfriend didn't exist and the pregnancy had never happened. She made me promise never to tell you.'

It seemed that she had relied on Andrew's loyalty as much as she had relied on mine. No wonder whenever I told her she should talk to Andrew about what Frank was doing to her, she would swear me to secrecy.

'Then she told me she was having an affair with this

Frank a couple of years ago,' he went on, 'but a bit later she admitted she'd made that up as well. She also told me about how she tied herself up to make it look like he'd done it. She said she did her wrists up with her teeth and then rang you. She showed me exactly how she did it.'

I noticed she hadn't added the detail that she had been naked when I found her, but I didn't want to dwell on that. How, I wondered, had she managed to give herself all the black eyes and split lips if she had made up all the beatings? They had made her stories so convincing. I didn't quite have the nerve to ask Andrew about that.

'You know, she worked as a nanny when she was a teenager,' Andrew continued.

From all the many thousands of hours of conversations that Tanya and I had had over the years, I remembered her telling me about how she was a nanny to a family somewhere around London. She was seventeen at the time and had had to leave because Frank had turned up and interfered with the little girl she had been looking after.

'Yes,' I said, wondering what was coming next. 'She did tell me that. Was it true?'

I had worked out that part of her skill as a storyteller had been that she always ensured there was at least a small element of truth in each tale, however far she might then stretch it in order to hold my attention.

'Did she tell you that she got into trouble with the family she worked for, for making up stories about a boyfriend beating her up? Apparently that boyfriend didn't exist either, and she damaged her own face with a scouring pad to make it look like she had been attacked.'

'No,' I said, 'she didn't tell me that.'

How did Tanya manage to keep track of all her lies, and who knew what? Her fantasies must have obsessed her to the point where perhaps she actually began to believe them. She was certainly convincing, with her attitudes of entirely realistic grief and bouts of despairing weeping.

None of that changed the fact that she had completely and utterly deceived me. How could I have been so easily fooled for so long? I had always prided myself on being a good judge of people and these revelations made me question every assumption I had ever made about myself. When I looked back and thought about everything she had told me, I couldn't understand how I swallowed everything she had said without question. Seen in its entirety, the story became ridiculous. How could one person have suffered so much and so often – in total secrecy? Why did I believe that just about everyone Tanya met was a rapist and sexual pervert? Why didn't I think it unlikely she had had so many children? On one occasion she had told me that she was attacked by two people just before she gave birth to the stillborn child, a woman holding her down while the man raped her. After the baby was delivered, she said, racked with heartbreaking sobs, they had forced her to break its bones and bury it in the garden. On another occasion, she said, her illegitimate grown-up son had tracked her down, forced her to tie herself up and raped her. Once she reported that Frank had bitten off her clitoris in a frenzy of sexual violence and she even showed me a digital photo she had taken of the wound, which was, to my relief, too fuzzy to be able to make out. Everything she said I believed. Now I feel like a fool just writing it down, it is so evidently made up.

According to her, Tanya had queues of people waiting to rape and impregnate her, and I never doubted her for a second.

It is hard to explain how easy it was to believe her. She was so plausible and she spent fourteen years gradually building up and elaborating her stories. Each one led to the next, leading me further and further up the garden path. Perhaps if I had been a little less loyal and had told someone else, even Mike, I might have started to realise just how ludicrous they were, but the way she fed them into my head always seemed so logical. There was always a reason for everything and an answer to every doubt or question I might raise.

In my defence, she fooled a lot of other people in different ways, and no one else worked out what she was up to. Because I spent so much time with her, and kept her revelations to myself over those years, never getting any perspective on them, Tanya had been able to suck me into her fantasy world and make me as deluded as she was, just as her therapist had warned me. My only possible excuse is that there were so many stories, I wasn't always listening actively when she told me a new one, but just nodded along. And I grew so used to the world she described where everyone was a sexual predator of some sort, that I lost touch with reality a bit when she was around.

Had I just once stepped back and asked myself if it was likely that one person would have lived such an extraordinarily jinxed life, and yet still managed to have a husband, two children and a home, while at the same time keeping up an appearance of normality, the whole thing would have collapsed. But she never gave me enough space to think about it rationally, and if ever I came up with an inconsistency in her stories that puzzled me, she was always quick with a plausible answer. I had to face it; she had made a fool of me for fourteen years.

I was tired of thinking about Tanya. Everything she had said and done had taken up so much of my brain for so long I was exhausted. All I wanted now was to retreat into my home with my lovely family and lock the rest of the world safely outside, at least for a while.

30

The Court

The case was finally heard a year after Tanya's confession. I was sitting waiting at the courthouse when Tanya turned up that morning. She didn't see me, but I saw her. She was laughing at something in her coat that had set off the metal detectors, looking confident and pleased with herself. Once she had passed the security, she strode up to the desk and gave her name, asking which court she was due to be in.

She looked so at home being at the centre of the judicial process, as if it was her natural place. I suppose I had expected her to look ashamed or embarrassed, perhaps even a little scared and overawed by what might be about to happen to her. But she was none of these things; she was in her element.

As she turned from the desk, her eyes passed over me. I saw a flicker of recognition, but only because I knew her so well; no one else would have spotted it. She recovered her composure immediately, staring straight through me as she swept away towards her next performance. It was as if she had no idea who I was, as if I had never been any part of her life, as if I had no relevance to whatever it was she was going to do and say that day.

I had been told that the judge who was presiding over the case was one of the tough ones. He certainly had a forbidding presence as he walked into the courtroom. Tanya was charged with assault occasioning actual bodily harm against Sarah, which covered the psychological abuse Sarah had suffered. There were also two charges of theft and two charges of harassment — one against myself and one against Sarah. The harassment charge included the criminal damage Tanya had inflicted on our home and possessions, and the mental torture she had put us through. She pleaded guilty to all the charges and the proceedings opened with a barrister speaking on behalf of the prosecution. He recapped what had happened since Tanya's first court appearance more than three months earlier, when the case was adjourned for psychiatric reports.

'This is an extraordinary case on the one hand,' he said, 'and sinister and shocking on the other, and with considerable long-term effects, not only for one person, but for many.'

He explained to the judge that our two families had been friends since before the children were born, and went on to talk about the disappearing money and the ripped clothes and curtains. He estimated that, in the end, more than a hundred different items had been damaged and cut, even mentioning a hole that was mysteriously punched through our shower curtain after we had locked up all the knives and scissors.

He explained how the authorities had started to believe that the whole thing was something to do with me, and how they put my relationship with Mike 'under the microscope', as he put it. It was strange to hear our lives talked about and to have to remain silent. It felt as though they were discussing someone else and the story sounded all the more shocking for that.

It only took the prosecution barrister half an hour to put his case, and then it was the turn of Tanya's lawyer. He didn't even start to pretend that Tanya hadn't done virtually everything she was accused of. There were a few things she denied, like the picture with the daggers in and some of the incidents with the tablets, but even if she was innocent of those there were more than enough other things to paint an accurate picture of just what hell she had put us through. All he could hope to do was try to explain why she had done such a terrible thing, in the hope that the judge would feel sorry for her and make some allowances when it came to sentencing.

He talked about how unhappy she and Andrew had been at home and suggested that financial difficulties had driven her to stealing the money from the Christmas Club. He explained that initially she only started to frame Sarah in order to divert suspicion from herself, and that was when 'the first seeds of what was to develop were sown'.

He talked about Tanya's sister, suggesting that Tanya was always 'in the shadows'. 'Over the years,' he said, 'she had developed a need to be wanted and to be important to somebody.'

He suggested that this need had been at the heart of why she enjoyed the feeling when I turned to her for help and advice about Sarah. I had inadvertently made her feel important and 'of worth'. He thought she had a 'compulsion' to hang on to her friendship with me.

'It was the relationship with Mrs Harris,' he concluded, 'that was the focus that she had, which blinkered her to all else that was going on.'

Tanya was claiming that as soon as she heard I had fallen under suspicion and the authorities were suggesting that I had Munchausen's syndrome by proxy and planned to take the children away from me, she realised she had to come forward and confess. Her barrister was hoping that the fact she had come forward voluntarily would go in her favour, along with the fact that she hadn't immediately gone looking for lawyers to protect her but had confessed freely and honestly.

'She would invite Your Honour to accept that she had remorse,' he said, 'and she is thoroughly ashamed of what she has done.'

I found it very hard to keep myself from shouting out once or twice during the proceedings, when I thought they had got things wrong; Holly was sitting three rows away and was still able to hear me muttering 'bollocks'. The judge, however, despite his fearsome reputation, was very lenient with me. It seemed as if he sympathised with what we had been through and was willing to turn a deaf ear to a bit of righteous indignation.

Tanya's barrister said he had letters for the judge and for me from Tanya, which she hoped we would read.

The judge took his, but didn't open it, while Holly intercepted the one on its way to me, not wanting me to open it in court, in front of everyone, without knowing what was in it.

When it came time for the judge to pass his sentence, he had observations of his own to make.

'The story of this case,' he said to Tanya, 'almost defies belief. It is a story of conduct on your part that can only be described as "wicked". I do not believe that I have previously dealt with a case which matched this one for pure wickedness.'

He went on to say that he thought her actions were those of 'a warped and twisted mind'.

'The strain that was placed upon the child's parents was enormous, and all the while you continued the pretence that you were a concerned friend, offering advice and help to two desperate parents. They were beside themselves with worry, yet you continued the pretence of friendship. You betrayed them and the trust they obviously placed in you. Quite simply, you watched them suffer.'

He said that it would be difficult to exaggerate the appalling consequences of her behaviour.

'I have read a number of reports,' he went on. 'Nothing that I have read would or could begin to excuse your behaviour, and I remain entirely sceptical as to whether the expert report begins to explain your conduct.'

He finished by handing down two sentences, one of a year for the theft and harassment and the other of three years for her assault on Sarah, to run concurrently.

I was so enormously relieved, it felt as though a burden had been lifted from me. I hadn't been wrong; Tanya's acts were wicked. I felt vindicated: it wasn't just me making a fuss about nothing. The legal system and an eminent judge agreed with me. I knew Sarah would be pleased Tanya was going to jail, even though she would feel sorry for Amy and David, because she had been punished herself for eighteen months and she could see clearly that everyone now believed her and felt she deserved to be recompensed.

When we got outside, Holly gave me a huge hug. It was as much of a triumph for her as it was for us. She had believed in us from the beginning and had worked hard to get a result that would be fair and would reflect the damage that had been done.

'Do you want the letter from Tanya?' she asked.

'No, chuck it away,' I said. Then I thought about it. I changed my mind. 'No. Hold on to it; I might read it later.'

A few days later, my curiosity got the better of me

and I asked Holly if I could have it. I opened it and read what Tanya had to say to me. She wrote how remorseful she felt and how sad that she had lost my friendship. She said she hoped that if she were sent to prison, it would go some way to making me feel better. She thanked me for treating her children no differently and for realising none of it was their fault – 'unlike some people'. The letter said all the right things, but it didn't sound like her somehow, more like a lawyer. In the end, it left me untouched. I just couldn't believe a word she said ever again.

'Who wrote the letter then?' I asked Andrew when I next saw him.

'Her sister helped her a bit,' he admitted.

I quite often talked to Andrew and David. They told me that Tanya seemed more interested in how many newspapers and magazines had covered the story than in how any of the rest of us were. She was probably disappointed because a big news story pushed our little drama right off the front pages. She always enjoyed being the centre of attention.

———

At last, it was over. This whole sorry affair had engulfed us for so long but now it had been set to rights. When I went over it all again, I thought that I could perhaps see why Tanya had done what she had, in a funny way. When David had gone off the rails, I had been her constant support as she wept and wailed and wondered why her boy was doing such terrible things. I had watched as social services had tried to help, and I had given her a shoulder to cry on. Perhaps she envied me my stable children and my placid husband and my ever-listening ear. Perhaps she literally wanted to reverse our roles, so that I had the problem child and angst about my mothering ability, and she was the calm, wise, patient friend.

Perhaps. We will never know. I don't even know if Tanya herself really understands why she did it. And one thing is for sure, I wouldn't believe her, whatever she said. My trust in her is too damaged.

———————

But, finally, we could go back to being a happy family.

Epilogue

The holiday in Spain, which I booked almost as soon as
the kids and I got back from Tenerife, came a few months
after Tanya's confession. Mike not only came with us, he
really enjoyed himself. For the two of us, it was like a
new beginning. The horrendous burden had been lifted,
and at last we could be a family again, and, just as importantly, a couple again. We were able to start communi-
cating and to begin patching over the gap that had grown
between us. There's nothing like getting away from
home to let you see things from a new perspective, and
it did us the world of good. The kids wanted to spend
nearly the whole week in the swimming pool, which

suited Mike as it meant he didn't have to go shopping. It was such a success we booked to go to Turkey for two weeks a year later, which allowed us to get away after the trial. It felt so wonderful to know that the worst was behind us and to watch Sarah and Luke behaving like normal kids.

Although Sarah has proved herself to be incredibly robust, there is no doubt that the events of that terrible time have left scars. Between the confession and the trial, Sarah talked a lot about Tanya. At Christmas, particularly, the memory of the disastrous Christmas Eve a year before was still painfully fresh in her mind. For some time after the revelation she would have nightmares and wake up screaming, terrified that Tanya was under her bed.

'You don't have to worry,' I would assure her as I cuddled her. 'She isn't coming near this house ever again.'

'I don't like it,' she would whimper. 'I feel she's going to get me.'

One day Sarah was a little concerned when she came home after her teacher had been talking about forgiveness in their religious studies class, telling the children that it would make them better people if they could be forgiving of others.

'I have to forgive Tanya, don't I?' she said. 'Otherwise I'm just as bad as she is.'

Epilogue

'Just because you can't forgive Tanya doesn't mean you are a bad person,' I assured her. 'She's done a very awful thing to you and it takes a lot to forgive something like that. You have every right to be angry with her.'

I always want to try to get some good from any bad situation, and I would like to think that those terrible eighteen months have had the effect of bringing us closer together as a family and making us appreciate more what we have.

'Do you think this experience has brought us closer together?' I asked Luke one day, when it was just the two of us together.

He looked thoughtful for a moment. 'Yes,' he said eventually, 'I think we're really close now.'

I'm so proud of them both and the way they have stuck by one another through such difficult times. Everyone can see how Sarah suffered, but Luke, too, had to put up with a lot, and he handled it all with amazing maturity for one so young. They are brilliant children and Mike and I are as proud as we can be.

'Although I hate her and what she's done,' Sarah told me one day, 'I still miss the old Tanya, the one that used to love me.'

I knew what she meant because, in a way, so did I. You can't have someone play that big a part in your life for that many years and not feel there is a hole when they suddenly disappear. But although I sometimes miss having Tanya around, it's also a relief to be free of a friendship that had become so stifling. Towards the end I used to dread her phone calls, knowing that they would bring some new trauma and I would have to listen for hours and provide her with moral support. It got to the stage where I was frightened to answer the phone, and I would get Mike to tell her I'd gone to bed or was in the bath. Now, without Tanya to occupy so many of my waking hours, I have so much more free time for myself and for my family.

Since it all ended, I have spent a lot of time having therapy myself, trying to understand how my own personality works. I understand that there is something that makes me want to feel needed, and that my desire to feel I am helping others is far stronger than my instincts, which are often right. I know now I must listen to my instincts more, and trust them. I realise that I got things badly wrong, and am partly responsible for what happened, which has been very hard to deal with.

I am making positive progress and can stand back more, resisting the need to sort out other people's problems all the time. I am happier now to be on my own from time to time, and I understand that my family is the most important thing in my life. Nothing else even comes close, or will ever be allowed to again.

———————

Wanting to make right everything that went wrong, I made a big effort to change our family patterns of behaviour. I went out and bought some family games to play together, instead of us all staring at television and computer screens in different parts of the house. We gave it our best shot, but I have to say, I couldn't see the attraction. Sarah sulked because she never won, Luke crowed because he did, and I just ended up getting cross with all of them. I suppose it's positive that the therapists and psychologists made me think about the way we run our family, but then again, as it turned out, there actually wasn't anything going that wrong in the first place.

Maybe I wasn't quite as disastrous as a parent as I always feared. I hope not. I have a feeling we are just a normal family after all.

Acknowledgements

To my mum and dad, brother and sister: thank you for all your love and support.

To Caroline and Mel: without you two I don't think I would have stayed so sane.

To Caithrin: thanks for giving me the courage to believe in myself. You never pretended to have the answers. Thank you for helping us to recover from what happened.

Nicci, thank you for making a really awful time much easier to deal with. You kept me fully informed, and always had time to answer my many questions. Your dedication ensured the best possible outcome.

Andrew, thank you from the bottom of my heart; you have put my thoughts and feelings into words. It was much better than I could have hoped for. You understood me which is never easy to do.

The biggest acknowledgement is to Mike, Sarah and Luke. We are a strong family, we got through a terrible time and we haven't let it break us. We are a stronger, more loving family because of it. We can learn something positive. She hasn't won.

Little Girl Lost

Barbie Probert-Wright with Jean Ritchie

Two sisters. A broken childhood. A heartbreaking journey.

In 1945, seven-year-old Barbie and her sister Eva were trapped, terrified, in war-torn Germany. With their father missing, and hundreds of miles from their mother, news of the approaching army left them confronted with an impossible choice: to face invasion, or to flee on foot.

Eva, aged nineteen, was determined to find her mother. For Barbie, twelve years younger, the journey was to be more perilous but, spurred on by her sister's courage and her desperate desire to be reunited with her mother, she joined Eva on a journey no child should ever have to endure.

Over three hundred miles across a country ravaged by a terrible war, they encountered unimaginable hardship, extraordinary courage and overwhelming generosity. Against all the odds, they survived. But neither sister came out of the journey unscathed . . .

Shattered

Mavis Marsh with Andrew Crofts

Sometimes a family's love can achieve the impossible . . .

On 12th October 1995, Mavis Marsh was woken to the news every parent dreads most. 'It's your son,' the policeman told her. 'He's been in an accident.' Only hours earlier Matthew had been set for a dazzling future but, in one terrible night, a devastating tragedy altered everything.

Days later, Mavis found herself standing at her son's bedside as doctors told her to give up all hope. According to them, the damage to Matthew's brain was too severe for him to recover, and the boy she had known and loved was gone forever.

But Mavis and her husband Keith couldn't give up on their only son. And refusing to accept the diagnosis, they started to work with Matthew themselves, desperately urging their comatose son to fight. For months they tried, to no avail. But then, almost half a year later, he suddenly started to respond . . .